D0102807

WAR ON TERROR:
The Middle East Dimension

Edited by Robert B. Satloff

Proceedings of the
2001 Weinberg Founders Conference

THE WASHINGTON INSTITUTE FOR NEAR EAST POLICY

© 2002 by The Washington Institute for Near East Policy

Published in 2002 in the United States of America by The Washington Institute for Near East Policy, 1828 L Street NW, Suite 1050, Washington, DC 20036.

Library of Congress Cataloging-in-Publication Data

War on terror: the Middle East dimension / Robert B. Satloff, ed.
    p. cm.
ISBN 0-944029-77-9
1. Terrorism—Middle East. 2. Terrorism—Middle East—Prevention. 3. September 11 Terrorist Attacks, 2001. 4. War on Terrorism, 2001- 5. Terrorists—Middle East. 6. United States—Foreign relations—Middle East. 7. Middle East—Foreign relations—United States. I. Satloff, Robert B. (Robert Barry)

HV6433.M5 C35 2002
303.6'25'0956—dc21
                                                    2002003116
                                                    CIP

Photo (left) of Islamic militiamen of the Asbat al-Ansar group burning the American flag near Sidon, Lebanon, October 24, 2001; photo (center) of smoke and flames billowing from a tour bus following a gun and bomb attack by suspected Islamic militants in front of the Egyptian Museum in Cairo, September 18, 1997; and photo (right) of rescue workers approaching the Sbarro pizzeria in Jerusalem following a suicide bombing by a member of the Palestinian terrorist group Hamas, August 10, 2001 © AP Wide World Photos. Color photo of explosion © Corbis. Cover design by Alicia Gansz.

The 2001 Weinberg Founders Conference was convened at the Lansdowne Conference Center in Leesburg, Virginia, October 19–21, 2001. This conference was made possible through a generous endowment gift by Barbi and Larry Weinberg.

Table of Contents

Introduction

I

T IS AN UNDERSTATEMENT to say that the attacks of September 11, 2001, were transformative events, both for how Americans view their own sense of security and for how America engages with the world. Osama bin Laden may have declared war on the United States years ago, but it was only on this date that the United States recognized the enormity of the war being waged upon it.

Still, as President George W. Bush stated in his address to the nation on September 20, 2001, "Our war on terror begins with al-Qaeda, but it does not end there. It will not end until every terrorist group of 'global reach' has been found, stopped, and defeated." And, he continued, in launching the strikes against Afghanistan on October 7, 2001: "Today we focus on Afghanistan, but the battle is broader. Every nation has a choice to make. In this conflict, there is no neutral ground. If any government sponsors the outlaws and killers of innocents, they have become outlaws and murderers themselves."

Although the current battle is being fought in central and south Asia, these principles—which constitute what can be called the Bush Doctrine—have special resonance in the Middle East. This region is home to organizations that share both ideology and methodology with the perpetrators of September 11, and to state sponsors of such groups of "global reach." It is the region in which bin Laden targeted his immediate operational objectives—that is, evicting American presence from the Arabian peninsula and overthrowing the regimes in Riyadh, Cairo, and Amman. And it is the region in which he has sought popular sympathies through an appeal to the Palestinian cause and through the atavistic call to expel Jews, Christians, and "Crusaders."

Focusing on the Middle East dimension of the campaign against terrorism is timely and urgent for reasons that go beyond al-Qaeda's local connections. There are aspects of the threat to U.S. interests that are particular to this part of the world: the frightening spread of weapons of mass destruction and their means of delivery; the ongoing challenge to the international system posed by Iraq; and, perhaps most of all, the reluctance that many U.S. allies in the region exhibit in confronting their own religious militants and in countering messages of intolerance that are standard fare.

In October 2001, just days after the shocking attacks on the World Trade Center and Pentagon, The Washington Institute convened its annual Weinberg Founders Conference to address the Middle East dimension of the war on terror. Over the course of three days, key U.S. and Middle Eastern scholars, experts, diplomats, journalists, and decisionmakers came together to examine and debate such themes as the common interests that regional states have in cooperating against terrorism; the different strategies that regimes have adopted in dealing with their Islamist challenges; the impact of September 11 on the Israeli-Palestinian arena; the problems and prospects of maintaining the antiterror coalition; and the role of democracy as an antidote to the region's ills. This edited volume includes the individual remarks and panel discussions from that conference. Taken together, these presentations provide valuable context for understanding the regional implications of the U.S.-led antiterror campaign, along with the ramifications of that campaign for U.S. policy in the Middle East.

Robert B. Satloff

Contributors

Khaled Abu Toameh is a senior writer for the *Jerusalem Report,* a special correspondent for *U.S. News & World Report,* and the Palestinian affairs producer for NBC. His previous positions include correspondent and analyst for Jerusalem Radio.

Gilles Andréani served in a series of posts in the French Ministry of Foreign Affairs, including director for disarmament issues, deputy permanent representative to NATO, and head of the Policy Planning Staff. He is currently a senior auditor in the Cour des Comptes and associate professor of International Relations at Paris II University.

Moshe Arens is currently a member of Israel's parliament (Knesset) from the Likud. In his distinguished public service career, he has served as Israel's minister of defense, minister of foreign affairs, ambassador to Washington, and chairman of the Foreign Affairs and Defense Committee of the Knesset.

Ami Ayalon served as director of Israel's domestic intelligence and security agency, the Israel Security Agency (Shin Bet), from 1996 to 2000. A career naval officer, he rose to admiral and commanded Israel's navy.

Samih Buttikhi served from 1996 to 2000 as head of Jordan's General Intelligence Directorate. In 1999–2000, he served concurrently as advisor to King Abdullah. He is currently a member of the Jordanian Senate, the appointed Upper House of Parliament.

Patrick Clawson is director for research at The Washington Institute and senior editor of *Middle East Quarterly.* An economist and specialist on Iran, he served previously as senior research professor at the Institute for National Strategic Studies of the National Defense University and as a research economist at the International Monetary Fund and the World Bank.

Mamoun Fandy is professor of politics at the Near East–South Asia Center for Strategic Studies at the National Defense University. His research focus is the politics of the Muslim world, with special interest in North Africa, the Arabian Gulf, and South Asia. His publications include *Saudi Arabia and the Politics of Dissent* (1999).

Leon Fuerth is a visiting professor of international relations at George Washington University's Elliot School of International Relations. A close advisor to Al Gore for the past twenty years, he served as national security advisor to the vice president throughout the Clinton-Gore administration.

Roger Harrison is academic chair of the Near East–South Asia Center for Strategic Studies at the National Defense University. A career foreign service officer, he served as political counselor in Tel Aviv, deputy political counselor in London, deputy assistant secretary of state for politico-military affairs, and ambassador to Jordan (1990–1993).

Amy W. Hawthorne is a senior fellow at The Washington Institute, focusing on U.S. democracy promotion in the Arab world. Previously, she was senior program officer for the Middle East at the International Foundation for Election Systems, a Washington-based democracy assistance organization. She managed programs in elections, rule of law, and women's political participation in the West Bank/Gaza, Morocco, Yemen, and the Gulf.

Ibrahim Karawan, a former Ira Weiner fellow at The Washington Institute, is associate professor of political science and director of the Middle East Center at the University of Utah. A former researcher at the al-Ahram Center for Strategic Studies in Cairo, he also served as senior fellow for Middle East studies at the International Institute for Strategic Studies in London, for whom he wrote the monograph *The Islamist Impasse* (1997).

Martin Kramer is editor of *Middle East Quarterly*, past director of the Moshe Dayan Center for Middle Eastern and African Studies at Tel Aviv University, and an internationally respected expert on Islamic history and politics. A former Ira Weiner fellow at The Washington Institute, he is the author of *Ivory Towers on Sand: The Failure of Middle Eastern Studies in America* (The Washington Institute, 2001).

Flynt Leverett, at the time of this conference, was a member of the State Department's Policy Planning Staff, covering Arab-Israeli issues and counterterrorism. Previously, he was a senior Middle East analyst and charter member of the Senior Analytic Service at the Central Intelligence Agency's Directorate of Intelligence. He is currently the director of Arab-Israeli affairs at the National Security Council.

Bernard Lewis is the Cleveland E. Dodge professor emeritus of Near Eastern Studies at Princeton University. Recognized around the world for his scholarship on the history of Islam and Islam's engagement with the West, his most recent book is *What Went Wrong? Western Impact and Middle Eastern Response* (2001).

Uri Lubrani, an advisor to the Israeli minister of defense, served from 1983 to 2000 as the government's coordinator for Lebanon affairs. In his long career, Mr. Lubrani served as ambassador to Uganda, Rwanda, Ethiopia, and Iran, as well as chairman of the Israeli delegation to the bilateral talks with Lebanon following the Madrid peace conference.

Kanan Makiya, an architect by training, is the founder of the Iraq Research and Documentation Project and author of *The Republic of Fear* (1989), *Cruelty and Silence: War, Tyranny, and Uprising in the Arab World* (1993), and a novel on Muslim-Jewish relations, *The Rock: A Tale of Seventh-Century Jerusalem* (2001).

Judith Miller is a senior writer at the *New York Times*, specializing in national security issues. A former Middle East correspondent for the *Times*, she is the author of *God Has Ninety-Nine Names: Reporting from a Militant Middle East* (1996) and, most recently, the coauthor of *Germs: Biological Weapons and America's Secret War* (2001).

Abdul Raouf al-Reedy capped his distinguished diplomatic career as Egypt's ambassador to the United States. He is currently chairman of the Mubarak Library and a member of the board of directors of the Egyptian Council on Foreign Relations.

Dennis B. Ross is the Ziegler distinguished fellow and counselor at The Washington Institute. In government, he served as special Middle East coordinator in the Clinton administration, director of the State Department's Policy Planning Staff in the first Bush administration, and special assistant to the president for Near East/South Asia affairs in the Reagan administration.

Robert B. Satloff is executive director of The Washington Institute. An expert on Arab and Islamic politics as well as U.S. Middle East policy, his many published works include *U.S. Policy toward Islamism: A Theoretical and Operational Overview* (2000).

Ehud Ya'ari is chief Middle East commentator for Israel's Channel Two, associate editor of the *Jerusalem Report*, and an associate of The Washington Institute. The winner of Israel's prestigious Sokolov Prize for coverage of the Lebanon war, his many published works include *Israel's Lebanon War* (1984) and *Intifada* (1989), both coauthored with Ze'ev Schiff.

PART ONE

Fighting Terrorism:
Lessons from the Front Lines

1

Ami Ayalon

IN THEIR SCOPE, the September 11 terrorist attacks were unprecedented. In the eyes of many, they represent the beginning of a new era. But despite the unique character of these attacks, what can the United States learn from the experience of others as it embarks on its own campaign against terrorism?

I oppose superficial analogies; every situation has distinctive features. Nonetheless, I take the liberty of viewing the American case from the perspective of my own personal experience. I was involved in the fight against terrorism as a commander in the Israel Defense Forces and as the head of the Israel Security Agency from 1996 to 2000. My remarks are based on the lessons I learned from both the successes and the many failures during that struggle.

For a military person like myself, the phenomenon of terrorism is difficult to understand. The military is accustomed to wars between armies involving generals and troops—or, in my case, admirals and ships. For us, the process of shifting to a fight against terrorism is a strange and frustrating experience. I will not embark on a long, academic discussion of the subject. Rather, I will quote the remarks of Shaykh Ahmed Yasin, founder of the Palestinian Hamas movement, from a press interview that he gave a few years ago: "The Israelis are very foolish. They believe that advanced technology will bring them victory. They cannot understand that, in the fight between us, the side that shows greater determination and faith will win."

According to Shaykh Yasin, the conflict between us is unlike the wars we have fought in the past; it is unlike the wars with which we are familiar. This war uses a different language, different reasoning, and different means—as well as different parameters for measuring achievements, victory, or defeat. We should not regard this war as an external threat, violent and brief. Instead, we should see it as an extended battle that has internal, erosive powers—something like a

3

concussive process, in which the whole of society takes part. Terms such as "victory" and "unconditional surrender" are not part of its lexicon. This fight exposes all the limitations of military and political power, and it sheds light on the negative side effects of using military power.

The fight against terrorism is part of a vicious cycle. The fight itself creates additional refugees, greater poverty, frustration, and despair, as well as greater humiliation and hate—leading to even more frustration and despair, more terrorism, and increased violence. According to Shaykh Yasin, terrorism—just like the fight against terrorism—is a way of life; it is not a fleeting battle that ends in either victory or defeat.

In the war against terrorism, the foundations of a democratic society are put to the test—especially the balance between security and freedom. Generals and admirals should not be conducting this battle. It is a complex campaign requiring the analytical skills and perceptions that distinguish politicians and statesmen.

Israelis generally consider the fight against terrorism in the years 1997–98 to have been successful. That fight was indeed crowned with amazing success. The number of victims decreased. The number of terrorist attempts decreased. The number of successes in preventing attacks increased. Looking at the background of this period, we see that a coalition was formed that achieved remarkable results in the fight against Palestinian terrorism. Members of this coalition were the Palestinian Authority's security services, the Israeli security services, the security and intelligence services of our neighboring countries—Egypt and Jordan—and, of course, the American intelligence services. Later, we analyzed the accomplishments achieved by this short-lived coalition. We concluded that Israeli initiatives had certainly brought good results. Beyond that, a number of exceptional factors had contributed to the coalition's success. I will discuss some of these.

First, the Palestinians themselves were highly motivated to fight Palestinian terrorism. Second, the Palestinians were ready to coordinate their fight against terrorism with us and with the Americans. Third, the Egyptians and Jordanians were willing to commit themselves to fight terror and to help us in this arena. Lastly—and apparently unconnected to the other factors—the terror organizations were much less motivated to promote terror attacks during this period.

This last point generated particular interest, and we studied it further. At the beginning, we mistakenly thought that the combined effort of the coalition members was the key to undermining the power of terrorism—thus enabling us to defeat the terrorists. When we looked more closely, however, we saw that Palestinian society itself was actually preoccupied with other questions at the time. It was dealing with issues of leadership and ideology, and was sorting out political objectives.

We concluded that, in great part, Palestinian policy toward terrorism—for or against—hinged on the political expectations of the Palestinian public. At certain points, the public saw the fight against terrorism as a legitimate step toward political independence—and was therefore willing to tolerate Palestinians fighting other Palestinians. This enabled the Palestinian security services to act to combat terrorism and coordinate their operations with us.

At other times, the public was disappointed by political developments and was ready to accept violence and terror as a legitimate component of the political process. At those times, the terror organizations—primarily Hamas—acted more freely. In this way, the Palestinian decision regarding whether or not to fight terrorism was tied to an internal debate within Palestinian society. And for us in Israel, the surveys conducted by Khalil Shikaki and Ghassan Khatib became important resources for predicting how much terrorist activity to expect; we used those surveys for intelligence research.

Thus, in 1997–98, a multinational coalition waged a relatively successful fight against Palestinian terrorism; but in my view, Palestinian public opinion made that successful fight possible. What lesson can we draw from this earlier experience as we engage in the current struggle? I will draw attention to some common elements.

First, public opinion plays a crucial role. In the current campaign, the pivotal public opinion issues relate to Islamic ideology. Some fundamentalist streams of Islam highlight the importance of individual education and faith. In contrast, Osama bin Laden and his al-Qaeda network are trying to instigate violent global terrorism as a means of provoking an internal Islamic revolution, an "internal jihad." In bin Laden's view, he is waging war on behalf of true Islam. The global revolution is secondary—its primary goal is to advance the internal Islamic process.

To bin Laden, a triangle of infidels comprises the enemy. The first component is, of course, the United States—the Western culture snake. The second is Israel, which controls Islamic holy places. And the third is made up of all the moderate Arab countries and regimes that do not accept radical Islam.

Al-Qaeda's fight today is—first and foremost—an attempt to achieve legitimacy in the Muslim world. It is an effort to develop from a small, marginal sect into a central stream of Islam. If al-Qaeda were to succeed in this effort—and were to enjoy the support of the masses—it would obtain several advantages. It would gain increased motivation to continue the Islamic revolution and to fight moderate Islam by violent means. And at the same time, moderate Islamic countries would have greater difficulty in fighting al-Qaeda or joining an outside coalition that is fighting the group.

For today's antiterrorism coalition, mobilizing Islamic public opinion is an essential element in the fight against terrorism. Economic assistance, sacks of flour, and medicine are important components—but they are not sufficient. A monumental debate is raging in the Muslim world over the direction that Islam will take in the face of globalization. In this debate, the Islamic public must hear the voice of moderation. Only leading personalities in the world of Islam—clerics and intellectuals—can participate. And those Islamic leaders who oppose the version of Islam that bin Laden advocates—internal jihad, global jihad, and terrorism—must participate vigorously. These leaders must play an active, not just passive, role in the fight against Islamic terror. They must be involved in the process of creating and upholding the coalition.

At the operational level, the antiterrorism coalition must refrain—as much as possible—from military operations that will lead to more refugees, poverty, and degradation. Exacerbating these problems breeds yet more hatred and terrorism, and thereby contributes to a vicious cycle. Therefore, I suggest that the coalition focus on specific targets and selective operations.

We should never forget that this is not the old kind of war to which we are accustomed. The criterion for measuring success is not whether we are able to prevent all terrorist attacks—we will not. Rather, the test is whether we will be able to continue living in an open, democratic society despite those attacks. At the end of the day, modernity and globalization will prevail. The only variable is the price we will ultimately pay in the nature of our democracies.

2

Samih Buttikhi

W E IN JORDAN WERE HORRIFIED by the vicious attacks on the World Trade Center and the Pentagon that claimed thousands of innocent lives. We were stunned by the orchestrated plot, which involved the hijacking of four large planes within minutes of each other. We anticipate a strong and effective response to these attacks. A broad international coalition has been forged, led by the United States and supported by the United Nations (UN). The war that will ultimately eradicate terrorism has commenced.

Several questions have surfaced concerning the suspects in these attacks. They were educated members of the middle class. Yet evil, hatred, and antagonism overpowered them—to the point that they were prepared to commit suicide and kill thousands of innocents in vicious terrorist acts. What could be driving these individuals, and others like them, to such a degree of hatred and antagonism? And why is the gap between the West and the rest of the world expanding?

Some in our region—and abroad—believe that Western dual policy in the Arab-Israeli conflict, along with the daily use of American weapons against Palestinians, constitute one reason for this hatred. Another problem is that—as people in the region see it—the West is holding more than 1 billion Muslims and 200 million Arabs responsible for September 11. Many fear that this Western response could enable the terrorists to achieve their ultimate objective—transforming the war against terrorism into an ethnic and religious war.

The anxiety among Muslims and Arabs is extremely high, particularly because the great majority of them condemn this evil attack. People are trying to define terrorism clearly. They are trying to differentiate between terrorism and resistance to occupation; they know that—at this time—only a thin line separates the two, especially when civilians are targeted.

Jordan was among the first countries to condemn the horrendous acts of September 11 and to announce its readiness to participate in the coalition. Indeed, Jordan has had its own experience with ter-

8

rorism. The founder of the Hashemite Kingdom, King Abdullah I, was killed in a terrorist act in 1951, because he advocated accepting a UN resolution that called for the partition of Palestine and peace between Arabs and Israelis. In addition, terrorists assassinated two of the kingdom's sitting prime ministers, and have also undertaken hundreds of other operations against Jordanian officials and foreign targets inside Jordan, as well as against Jordanian interests abroad—including diplomats and aircraft.

Globalization is breaking down barriers; let us cooperate to protect our world. Terrorism and extremism threaten progress, but good intelligence and international cooperation are our best weapons. Real partnership will protect our common global interests: pursuing progress, respecting human rights, assuring security, and maintaining the rule of law. In this context, we in Jordan have been open to cooperation. I am pleased to say that we have aborted several terrorist operations against Israelis, even prior to the 1994 Jordan-Israel peace treaty.

In addition, the Jordanian General Intelligence Directorate succeeded in thwarting the millennium terrorist operation. That operation—planned by Osama bin Laden's al-Qaeda organization—had targeted vital interests in Jordan, the United States, and elsewhere during the 1999–2000 New Year's celebrations. We arrested and prosecuted the perpetrators, and we seized the weapons and explosives they had intended to use in Jordan. Our effort ultimately saved the lives of hundreds of people, including Americans. In an address to the Coast Guard Academy on May 17, 2000, the president of the United States expressed his appreciation for the Jordanian effort.

Indeed, since the 1970s, Jordan has been warning of the threat posed by terrorism, and has been calling for multilateral cooperation on this issue. But these warnings went unheeded. Until now, the majority of Western countries considered terrorism a distant threat.

I participated in a counterterrorism conference—a summit of peacemakers—in Sharm al-Shaykh, Egypt, on March 13, 1996, and also in the follow-up experts conference held immediately thereafter in Washington, D.C. The Jordanians, along with others, tried to institutionalize counterterrorism and to deter regimes that support terrorism. We attempted to instate binding principles requiring each country to refrain from supporting terrorism and to find a mechanism for punishing violators. Sadly, both conferences failed to achieve any tangible results.

At the Sharm al-Shaykh conference, His Majesty, the late King Hussein, stated:

> Those who use religious justifications for terrorist acts have tarnished the image of Islam, which is a religion of peace, tolerance, and dialogue. A dual approach must be used in the fight against terrorism. Sources of funding, training, and operations must be cut off, and media coverage must not encourage terrorism—and we must eliminate those sources of despair that drive persons to perform such terrible actions.

The introduction I have just provided lays the foundation for my suggestions on how to deal with September 11. To minimize, if not eliminate, the possibility of a similar catastrophe, we must take short-, medium-, and long-term measures. In the short term, the military strike against Afghanistan, where bin Laden's terrorist bases are located, should continue. The objective should be to eliminate the Taliban regime—and al-Qaeda's presence—by destroying the physical infrastructure of the Taliban and disabling its organization. A new, moderate regime should continue the fight until the terrorist networks in Afghanistan are completely eradicated. Moreover, the new regime should be supported economically, to improve the living conditions of the Afghan people.

There is also the real possibility that sleeper cells remain in the United States, Canada, and Mexico—and perhaps in many other countries. They are waiting to respond to the strike against Afghanistan. We do not know how these cells will operate; different scenarios are possible. They could strike power stations, petrochemical plants, or crowded places such as shopping centers and athletic facilities. As far as their weaponry, I fear that the use of biological weapons is possible.

In his address to Congress on September 20, 2001, President George W. Bush made it very clear that this threat is not directed solely against the United States, but against us all. The president was right. Accordingly, the international community should continue to fight this war until the very end, and on all fronts—military, intelligence, security, economic, and political. We must learn from our past mistakes and not accept compromise. We should not stop even a few yards short of our goal. We should not differentiate, as we have in the past, between "global terrorism" and "regional terrorism." We should not tolerate "regional terrorism" under the pretext that it is confined to a specific place against a specific party, and therefore does not threaten the entire international community. (Applause.)

We have suffered the consequences of jobs left unfinished. We left Afghanistan to the armed extremist parties at the end of the Soviet invasion. We have allowed the Arab-Israeli conflict to continue without resolution. And we have wasted a whole decade in Iraq through fruitless policies and actions.

In the medium and long term, we must take action to extinguish the focal points of tension that generate terrorism. Achieving peace between the Israelis and the Palestinians, Syrians, and Lebanese is crucial to this end. Although comprehensive peace continues to be our objective, the Israeli-Palestinian track should be a high priority—for two reasons. First, it is the core of the conflict. Second, over the last twelve months it has deteriorated disastrously. This deterioration has made the situation on the ground extremely volatile, with the potential for grave, long-term consequences. In this context, resolving the affairs of the Palestinian refugees who will not be returning to their homeland following peace will be crucial; this issue constitutes a time bomb for everyone.

In addition, we will also have to deal with the disorder in Iraq, Chechnya, Kashmir, and other areas. We need an umbrella to unite the entire international community and institutionalize counterterrorism. We need a clearly written convention that provides a framework and mechanism for defining and targeting terrorism. In the context of that convention, we should also formulate a resolution to be put before the UN General Assembly and Security Council, in accordance with Chapter 7 of the UN Charter. The convention I envision would require states to:

- condemn all forms of terrorism;
- desist from supporting terrorism in any form and cooperate fully with the international community in efforts to combat it;
- dry out terrorist financial sources;
- hand over—or prosecute—wanted terrorists and provide information on terrorist organizations to an international data bank to be established by the UN;

- deny political and humanitarian asylum to terrorists;
- curb the propagation of extremism, which gives rise to terrorism; and
- enact legislation to enhance a state's ability to fight terrorism effectively—such as granting counterterrorism services more flexibility and eliminating bureaucratic obstacles to combating terrorism effectively.

Should the international community adopt this type of convention, it will be able to maintain a unified stance against violators—and it will be able to do so under the rule of law.

Before I move on, I would like to comment on some of the specific points in my proposal. I said that governments must dry out the sources of terrorism financing. In this effort, governments should pay special attention to the huge funds belonging to certain nongovernmental organizations—Islamic and non-Islamic—as a significant portion of these funds wind up in the hands of terrorists.

As for granting asylum to terrorists, terrorists often seek asylum under the pretense that they have been oppressed in their home countries. In many cases, these individuals are either wanted on suspicion that they have committed terrorist acts, or have already been prosecuted in their home countries for committing such acts. European countries often grant asylum to these individuals—maintaining that their laws permit asylum in such circumstances—as long as the terrorist actions were not directed against those countries themselves. Governments should not be permitted to use such legal pretexts to protect individuals who threaten the rights—and indeed the very lives—of others.

I spoke of the need to curb extremist propaganda. I refer especially to the Islamic schools that graduate thousands of extremists—and potential terrorists—including those running the Taliban regime.

I have laid out a plan for an effective international fight against terrorism. Although fighting terrorism is necessary, it is not sufficient. We must also address the poverty and despair that provide fertile breeding ground for terrorism. Some poor countries strive relentlessly to fight the evil of terrorism and to spread political, religious, and ethnic moderation and tolerance. They employ many resources in this effort. Supporting these countries and providing them with corresponding rewards is a very effective weapon in countering terrorism. I quote from an article that World Bank president James Wolfensohn published in the *International Herald Tribune* on October 6, 2001:

> The greatest long-term challenge for the global community in building a better world is that of fighting poverty and promoting inclusion worldwide. This is even more imperative now, when we know that because of the terrorist attacks, growth in developing countries will falter, pushing millions more into poverty and causing tens of thousands of children to die from malnutrition, disease and deprivation.

I would like to conclude by quoting His Majesty King Abdullah II: "We can win, if you, the United States of America, do not forget who you are, if you do not forget who your friends are, and if we work together."

PART TWO

Regime Strategies in the Middle East: The Role of Islamism, Anti-Americanism, and Terrorism

3

Martin Kramer

THERE IS AN OLD ADAGE that the first casualty of war is the truth. If offering up this casualty can spare real casualties in lives, it is worth sacrificing some truth. I heard it said the other day, by a very accomplished analyst of the Middle East, that this is not the time for too deep an analysis. There is something to be said for that: the focus must be on winning. Yet, it is still important to get basic assumptions right, and not to let certain untruths—let us call them myths—go unchecked for too long. Practicing certain economies of truth is supposed to handicap the enemy. But if these turn into our own myths, they could wind up handicapping us.

In that spirit, I want to focus on some myths that have emerged in the aftermath of September 11. Some myths, of course, have had a very short shelf life. I no longer see any need to explode the myth that September 11 was a protest against Israel. This myth flourished briefly in the first few days after the attacks, but now it has been relegated to the furthest margins of the public arena. Yes, most people think progress between Israelis and Palestinians would help. But very few believe that the actual attacks were motivated by the breakdown of the "peace process," especially as we know that September 11 was set in motion long before that breakdown. And few think that progress in the peace process would deter future attacks. The more we learn about this plot, the more it seems to have operated on several regional levels. September 11 certainly did not constitute a chapter in the Arab-Israeli conflict, and it seems to belong properly in another book.

Yet, two other myths have taken root, largely because they have arisen within influential quarters in this country. The first purports to explain the motives of the attackers; the second purports to interpret the reaction of the Arab world. These myths are already powerfully ensconced in the American understanding of September 11. Unfortunately, they are both dangerous. By misreading the terrorist motive and the Arab response, the United States, in the best instance, could cloud the objectives of this war. In the worst instance, it could effectively invite further terrorist attacks.

The first myth has to do with motive in the most general sense, and it has been propagated most effectively by a part of the media. Perhaps it reached fullest flower in the cover article of the October 15, 2001, issue of *Newsweek:* Fareed Zakaria's mega-essay "The Politics of Rage: Why Do They Hate Us?" In that piece, Zakaria argues that the failed states and collapsing societies of the Arab world are awash in resentment against the creativity, wealth, and democracy of the West. The success of America, and the influence radiated by that success, drives them to distraction—and to terrible deeds. The world's greatest losers, the Arabs, are seeking revenge against the world's greatest winners, the Americans. Francis Fukuyama has written something similar, and it can well be argued that this has become the preferred spin of those who think history has truly ended with the triumph of liberal democracy and capitalism. What we are dealing with, they seem to say, is a rearguard action by the losers in the great battle among organizing principles of humankind. Needless to say, by this analysis, we do flatter ourselves a bit.

I propose a different thesis. Yes, America is hated by many Muslims, and it is a reflection of their resentment against American success and power. But it is actually worse, because this rage against America is mingled with contempt—contempt for America's perceived weakness, a weakness most manifest in the Middle East. It is the contempt, not the hatred, which poses the immediate danger. And while you cannot do anything about the hatred—after all, it is a side effect of your success—you can and must do something to diminish the contempt.

Let me frame the question this way: are we certain that, in Arab and Muslim eyes, the United States really does look like the great winner? It is not difficult to see why Osama bin Laden and his cohorts have a rather different view. After all, they defeated another superpower, the Soviet Union, in Afghanistan. You think you won the Cold War. They think they won it. To them, the United States is a similar giant with similar feet of clay. And they summon their best evidence right from their doorstep in the Middle East.

The new contempt dates from the Iranian revolution, "Exhibit A" for American weakness. In Iran, Ayatollah Ruhollah Khomeini threw out the shah, held Americans hostage, sent his agents to kill Americans by the hundreds in Lebanon, and got away with it. Iran is a shining instance of successful defiance of the United States, evidence that you can run a major state in the region for more than twenty years completely outside the orbit of American influence. The list of most-wanted terrorists was published recently. Several of those on that list killed Americans sixteen years ago, and still roam free in Iran.

In the 1990s, the record was no better. Saddam Husayn crossed every line in the sand, spit in the face of the United States, and got pummeled in return—but still stands on his own two feet. Other Arabs may not have a lot of sympathy for Saddam. But he is living, breathing proof in their eyes that the United States never presses its advantage, that it remains highly "risk-averse" in the Middle East, that it does not always get its man, and that you can defy the last superpower and live to fight another day.

Do you remember the horror of Pan Am Flight 103? A single Libyan operative went to prison for this, while Muammar Qadhafi recently celebrated his thirty-second year in power. Perhaps removing Qadhafi would have been a very tall order. But what about removing the Somali warlord Muhammad Aideed, against whom a previous administration sent the Marines? It turned out that getting him was too tall an order as well.

Consider Osama bin Laden. He has been America's "most wanted" for years. Yet, aside from a few misguided cruise missiles, no serious operation was mounted against him until now. Many Muslims admire him not just because of what he says about the United States, but because the United States has not killed him yet. The bin Laden we saw in the most recent video was not spewing hate, he was displaying outright contempt, wagging his finger at America while sipping tea.

Perhaps there is rage against American power in these attacks. But there is even more contempt for America's weakness—its perceived lack of resolve; its quickness to forgive, or at least forget; its penchant for creating categorical boxes, like the state sponsors of terrorism list, and then ignoring them altogether. This is perceived as weakness, and when you are perceived as weak in the Middle East, you become a tempting target and the vultures begin to circle. Needless to say, the images of the Twin Towers in flames have only compounded the problem. America now appears still weaker, more vulnerable than ever.

But paradoxically, Americans seem almost too concerned with the hatred. America wants and even expects to be loved in the world. It wants to be admired and respected. And it is shocked to discover that in many quarters, it is hated. The desire to be loved, the bewilderment at being despised, are endearing American foibles. And it is curiously endearing to see American statesmen running to mosques, telling the world that Islam is a religion of peace—in the hope that this love will be returned.

But September 11 has to bring America to two realizations. First, while it is good to be loved and admired, it is more important to be feared. The United States is not sufficiently feared in the Middle East. If it wants to maintain its own interests or even simply deter attacks against its homeland, it will have to rectify that impression. And second, although no one likes to be the target of hatred, it is far worse to be the subject of contempt. Look, for example, at the suicide pilots, the men who spent long months, even years, here in America. What is striking is not their hatred for this country, but their contempt: the fact that America is so naively trusting of foreigners, that it gives everyone the benefit of the doubt, and that it is willing to sell the very training needed to destroy it.

The people in the streets of Karachi or Cairo who burn U.S. president George W. Bush in effigy are in a blind rage, but they are not dangerous. They do not know enough about America to be dangerous. The dangerous ones are like these suicide pilots—those who are familiar with America, who know where to find a Wal-Mart or how to get a credit card, whose idea of the "women of paradise" probably owes more to MTV than to anything they saw back in their dusty corner of Saudi Arabia. Their own familiarity with America has bred a deep contempt, far more deadly than impotent rage. The hatred will always be there. It comes with the turf, and it is the price of success. Get used to it. But contempt is another story. It is much more dangerous, and it will eat away at your deterrence.

Contempt can be banished, however, if you work at it. Let me summarize this way: nothing engenders greater respect in the Middle East than the rewarding of your friends and the certain punishment of your enemies. Over the past two decades, the United States has gained a reputation for inconsistency on both counts. And this has left America more vulnerable. American credibility cannot be reestablished overnight. But the United States has now been given an opportunity, a license, to rebuild it. It is the gift given by the thousands who perished, and it seems to me absolutely crucial that this second chance not be missed—not only if U.S. interests are to be defended abroad, but also if the American way of life is to be preserved at home.

And in the region, this means that you must smite your enemy in a decisive and demonstrative way. This requires two things. First, you must get rid of the Taliban regime. The United States has not deposed a regime in the Middle East in fifty years. It must do so now. Second, you must get Osama bin Laden—and not in one, two, or sixteen years. Every day he lives is an affront to American credibility.

Let me be clear: nothing you do will ever even the score for September 11. But do these two things, and you will rebuild the gaping hole left in your wall of deterrence. Do these two things, and you will create awe and fear among the multitudes. Fail, and you will engender derision and contempt—and the fear will be yours. Fail, and the "war on terror" could become something like the "war on drugs"—not a matter of a few years but of decades, a struggle waged indecisively against a succession of bin Laden impersonators who continue along the path of terror because the gains outweigh the risks, and in the end it pays off.

I come now to the second myth, regarding the Arab response. This myth has its origins not in the media but in government. It is best appreciated in a quotation from Secretary of State Colin Powell: "Out of a deep sense of shared humanity, and a chilling appreciation of common vulnerability to terrorism, we see new scope to strengthen our relations with the Islamic world."

No one can doubt all of our shared humanity, or that it includes the Islamic world. And no one can doubt that it is in America's interests to strengthen relations with the Islamic world. But I would like to focus on an assumption that I found perplexing: that the Arab world shares with America "a chilling appreciation of common vulnerability to terrorism." Or, as someone else put it, "Saudi and Egyptian support is not a favor to us; it is an act of self-defense." When I first read these arguments, I was perplexed, because something about them did not ring precisely true. Now, after more than a month of American diplomacy predicated on this assumption, I am more certain than ever that it is not true—and because it is false, any attempt to build a coalition on this assumption is destined to falter and fail.

Obviously, Osama bin Laden is a Saudi, and the perpetrators of the crimes in New York and Washington were Saudis and Egyptians. Bin Laden's network is made up primarily of nationals belonging to Arab countries in the Middle East. It is also true that this network would like to topple Arab regimes. But Osama bin Laden wound up in Afghanistan for a reason. And the reason, in a nutshell, is this: his brand of Islamic fundamentalism has been driven out of the Arab Middle East, where it has ceased to be much of a problem.

Bin Laden, Ayman al-Zawahiri, and the lot of them are in Afghanistan precisely because they failed in the Middle East. When the Afghan jihad ended, bin Laden and many other Arabs left Afghanistan to return to the region. Once in place, they did try to terrorize regimes, assassinate leaders, and seize power. But they failed. By the late 1990s, those regimes had them cornered. The rulers in the Arab world were not about to be terrorized out of their presidential or royal palaces, and they unleashed a massive counteroffensive. Egypt put some 50,000 fundamentalists in its prisons; hundreds went to the gallows. In Saudi Arabia, those who were not beheaded were exiled. Today, no Arab regime faces a credible threat from Islamist extremists.

In fact, what happened in New York and Washington was, to some extent, a consequence of the Arab success in pushing those like bin Laden to the margins. Since the extremists could not defeat the Arab regimes, they went over their heads and attacked the American patron of those regimes. Since they could not build a network in Saudi Arabia or Egypt without it being betrayed and its members sent off to torture chambers, they built networks in East Africa, and even in America itself.

Osama bin Laden and his crowd want to drive America from the entire Middle East in order to topple regimes. But they have no strong base in the region itself, nor can they easily strike there. So they have gone straight for the jugular—and there is no greater jugular than lower Manhattan.

This means that, at the moment, there is no one in the Middle East who shares a sense of "common vulnerability" to terrorism, except Israel. In the 1990s, the Arab states had a terrorism problem, and they got rid of it by the usual methods: mass arrests, torture, expulsions, "disappearances," and so on. These states are not threatened in any way by terrorism, which they have pushed out to Afghanistan and the West where it is somebody else's problem—above all, America's. In the region, there is some sympathy for bin Laden because he symbolizes defiance of the West. But only the smallest minority of Arabs would want to live under a Taliban-style regime. Actually, there seems to be less "turmoil" in the Arab street than there was during the Gulf War. The Arab world is riveted by the September 11 story, but so far it has not been moved by it.

The regimes are not threatened, and this is why the Arabs are not going to be very predictable partners in this coalition. Every time Americans sit down to talk to them about terrorism, they are going to want to talk about other things that really do worry them: what they want from Israel, how many weapons they need, how much their debts weigh on them, or how much they want for their oil.

One can understand why some American diplomats might look upon this "war on terror" as a possible theme around which to organize the Middle East. Right now, there is no organizing theme, and that is a problem. During the Cold War, the United States tried to organize the region on the basis of the Soviet threat, which inspired the Baghdad Pact, CENTO, and so on. This never worked particularly well, because the states of the region felt more threatened by one another than by the Soviet Union. After the fall of the Soviet Union and the Gulf War, the United States tried to organize the Middle East around the "peace process" and economic cooperation, the so-called "new Middle East." This, too, never quite worked, since Arabs feared it might become a form of veiled Israeli hegemony.

Now, some seem intent on organizing the region around the "war on terror," buttressed by the ancillary notion that America is the true defender of Islam. All of this is perfectly understandable, but let us be frank. The war on terror is shaky scaffolding for a new Middle East architecture—even shakier than the Soviet threat and the peace process. Already the Saudis are stonewalling, the Egyptians are balking—and these are America's friends. Arab governments do not need American help to fend off fundamentalist terrorism these days; they are looking for some bigger payoff before they get on board.

But even if the Arab governments were willing, and there were something to be gained from their cooperation, chasing after these fickle friends has a major downside: it signals that the United States needs the blessing of others before responding to an attack on its own territory. In essence, America is saying that even its own self-defense is legitimate only if it is approved by a "rainbow coalition," which ironically includes not a few veteran America-bashers. There is something unseemly in this image of the United States seeking the support of a lot of tin pots. If the United States smashes the Taliban and gets bin Laden, no damage will have been done. But if this whole grand coalition fails to meet minimal goals, it could contribute to the kind of contempt that made September 11 an appealing strategy in the first place.

These then, it seems to me, are two myths that must be challenged before the end of hostilities. The war's outcome must create awe and banish contempt. No amount of kowtowing to Islam can substitute for victory. And since America is going to win this war by itself anyway, victory should be made to look unquestionably like America's triumph, not the triumph of a gerrymandered coalition. The less credit you share, the more awe you will induce.

Finally, do not neglect your friends. There is an old adage: keep your friends close, and your enemies closer. Be careful not to confuse the two. Israel does not need to be a big cog in this coalition—the latter is unlikely to last very long anyway. But America will do itself more harm if it even appears to be shunning its friends. This will not produce more Arab respect; it will only invite more Arab contempt—adding to the problem, rather than subtracting from it.

The best guarantee that there will not be a next time is for America to rely on itself to win this war, and on its proven friends to build a common wall of deterrence. So far, the going has been easy in the American offensive against terror. At some point, it will get tough. When it does, the United States will find out who its real friends are. And on that day, it will need more than Arabic.

4

Ibrahim Karawan

THREE RECURRING THEMES have marred much of the recent analysis of terrorism. First, many analysts downplay the danger of Islamic militants by arguing that they represent a very small percentage of the Muslim population. This argument is specious; September 11 should be enough to illustrate that small can be lethal. In fact, the very logic underlying contemporary terrorism is that small numbers of people are difficult to identify, and their small number also gives them a sense of elitism—which in turn gives them a sense of mission.

In fact, a small band of terrorists can cause enormous damage. In Egypt, for example, just six individuals killed dozens of tourists at Luxor in 1997, and managed to reduce Egypt's annual growth rate by nearly one full percentage point; of course, the repercussions of that massacre cannot compare with the potential impact of September 11. Moreover, many terrorist groups enhance the destructive power of their small numbers by rotating their members, thereby complicating the process of identifying and tracking them. Most alarmingly, even the smallest terrorist group could inflict unprecedented damage if it obtained access to weapons of mass destruction. So, in assessing Islamic militancy, the argument that only a "small number" of Muslims are militants is not really helpful, because it fails to recognize the enormous impact that a few people can have.

Beyond that, if we focus on the methods that individuals employ to express their disagreement, we may discover that the true number of militants is larger than we realize. Given a choice between two people with whom I disagree ideologically—one who confronts my argument with a book, and one who confronts it with a machine gun—I would invariably choose the one with the book. There is a basic difference in human discourse between relying on words and relying on bullets. A fundamental, qualitative change occurs in political movements that switch from rhetoric to guns.

25

This distinction is complicated when some who are supposed to be ideologically or politically moderate offer verbal support for militancy. For example, Egyptian Shaykh Muhammad al-Ghazali of al-Azhar University appears to be an intelligent and presumably enlightened man; yet, he sanctioned the murder of my friend, Farag Foda, explaining that if the state does not put an end to behavior that is considered apostasy, true believers should take matters into their own hands. With moderates like that, who needs extremists? We need to look carefully at the statements of such individuals; they may be professing moderation, while actually sending quite a different message. We should pay special attention to statements they package for certain audiences, and to the mentality they promote during times of crisis. However difficult it may be, we must learn to distinguish between moderation and militancy—between what is dangerous and what is not.

A second recurring theme in recent commentary is the focus on the "root causes" of terrorism. Seeking to understand the sources of discontent in the Middle East is important. Yet, the argument that these sources constitute the causal root of terrorism often twists the truth. Certainly, terrorist acts must be viewed in context; the challenge is to interpret that context correctly. Is every disgruntled person in the world opposed to America and American policy? Does every person who abhors American policy fly airplanes into buildings full of innocent people?

Take, for example, those who blame the September 11 attacks on the stalled Arab-Israeli peace process. My own daughter, a student of philosophy at the University of California at Berkeley, recently asked me whether she should expect more of these attacks in the future if the Palestinian-Israeli talks hit another wall. This way of thinking elides the distinction between the motives of the terrorists and the attitudes of the general public in the Middle East.

As the United States considers making concessions in order to build a coalition against terrorism, it must be very careful to avoid such elision. Any concession must be based, among other things, on a careful determination of whether that concession is really necessary—and sufficient—to achieve the objective. America must also realize that any concession it makes for the purpose of building a coalition may do nothing whatsoever to deter terrorism. To paraphrase Dennis Ross, does anyone really believe that September 11 would have been averted if Bill Clinton, Ehud Barak, and Yasir Arafat had succeeded in their search for a settlement? Would such a settlement have deterred those who do not even recognize Israel's right to exist?

The root problems in the region should not be addressed merely out of political utility, but on their own merits. Anyway, these problems cannot be solved overnight, and focusing on them is not a viable means of dealing with terrorism in the short run. Moreover, terrorists are unlikely to be deterred by the probable Western approach to solving these problems—that is, the promotion of peace, economic development, and democratization in the region. The terrorists themselves would not implement these measures if they had the opportunity. It is ludicrous to justify al-Qaeda's attacks by pointing out, however correctly, that certain Arab regimes are oppressive and corrupt; al-Qaeda itself is working with the Taliban government, which is hardly a shining example of liberalism. The "root problems" of the Middle East are important in any discussion of terrorism; however, we must distinguish between causal factors and legitimizing factors, and we must avoid using language that justifies political positions but does not actually explain political action in a meaningful way.

A third theme in the media coverage of September 11 is a certain subliminal attitude of near admiration for the terrorists; I do not mean deliberate praise of the men themselves, but rather observations on how meticulously planned and fantastically successful their attacks were on the tactical level. In particular, commentators have focused on the terrorists' innovative and largely unforeseen use of civilian airplanes, and on the possibility that such a wily enemy may, in the future, devise other novel tactics that we would be similarly unable to guard against.

Yet, through these attacks, the terrorists have committed the same strategic mistake of "overextension" that the superpowers committed in the past. Overextension occurs when a country establishes a logical relationship between means and ends, between resources and obtainable objectives, and then imprudently breaks that link. The Soviet Union and the United States made this mistake on a number of occasions during the Cold War. Small, ideologically driven ethnic or religious groups can likewise make wrong strategic choices and land in this same trap of overextension. For example, Islamic terrorists will sometimes act under what some of them call *ghadhbatan li-allah,* a "rage for God"; they will do something without calculating its practicality, focusing instead on achieving an objective and provoking God to participate in the struggle. Although they may act under this "rage for God" in an attempt to remake reality in their own ideological image, in practice, they often end up creating more enemies, unleashing greater repression, and bringing other adverse consequences upon themselves.

September 11 is just such a case of overextension followed by consequences adverse to the terrorists' interests. The terrorists wanted to humble America, and indeed the attacks did cause embarrassment. Yet, throughout America and overseas, the September 11 attacks have also caused intense discussion about what made such attacks possible, and they have raised powerful new fears and concerns about what the terrorists might be able to do in the future. As a result, America, Western Europe, and other countries have implemented broad new efforts aimed at stymieing terrorism. Groups such as al-Qaeda may now find it very unfortunate to have brought that kind of intense attention upon themselves, as the resulting countermeasures may weaken their ability to move funds, recruit followers, and train quietly.

Successful exploitation of the terrorists' overextension will depend on a number of factors, including how determined the United States is; whether it relies more on its mind or on its muscle; and how well it can sustain its coalition. I would like to add a word about coalitions. The United States must realize that coalitions are not meant to be collections of states with identical positions on every issue. Leaders who join coalitions must be able to maintain a certain level of credibility within their own societies; if the United States asks its partners to be puppets, it will contribute to their undoing.

As for the titular subject of this panel, Islamism, I am in full agreement with Martin Kramer: Islamism is a stagnant phenomenon in the Arab world today. One would never know this, however, from reading or listening to Western scholars, writers, and analysts. They portray a very different picture—based on a kind of "touristic" scholarship. They go to Cairo or Amman, sit in coffee shops, and count how many female passersby are wearing scarves. If seven out of ten women are wearing scarves, these observers conclude that the Islamist Revolution is alive and well in that country. The same thing happens with internet cafes; the analysts make their count and then declare that the Information Revolution has triumphed in the Arab world.

Let me share a well-kept secret: neither the Islamist Revolution nor the Internet Revolution has prevailed in the Arab world. We must move beyond touristic scholarship. Arab leaders read this sort of analysis and laugh; they know that Islamism does not pose a significant threat to their regimes. This is not to say that Islamism is irrelevant to analyses of the Arab world today, but it is stagnant. Islamists have failed to achieve their most important goal—political power. They did not seek to become debating societies or philanthropic organizations; they wanted to gain political power. Indeed, that very goal defines the difference between a Muslim and an organized Islamist.

But the Islamist quest for political power has stagnated. We are now far past the era when the *New York Times* assembled every Islamic expert it could find in order to ask which Arab regime was on the brink of being overthrown by the Islamists. We no longer see such intensive public focus on that question because the threat has diminished. The Islamists themselves recognize this; they keep producing books with titles such as *What Went Wrong?* Yet, when I come to Washington, I find that the analysts have declared Islamism triumphant in Egypt, my home country. Their analysis contravenes reality.

Fouad Ajami once said, brilliantly, "If you lower your standards too much, anything will appear as an improvement." If you lower your standard for the "triumph of Islamism," you will always find proof to support your conclusion. But one need only look at the five roads to political power to see how poor Islamist prospects are in the Middle East. Terrorists have already tried one path—assassination—in a number of Arab countries; it did not bring them any closer to their goal. For example, they murdered Egyptian president Anwar Sadat, yet his system of governing—and his main policy orientation—lives on.

The second path to power is by military coup. In the 1980s, Israeli scholar Eliezer Be'eri, a highly regarded analyst of Arab military regimes, argued persuasively that using military coups to seize power in Arab states is much more difficult than it once was. The intervening years have only proven his point, particularly given the increased size of modern Arab armies. We are past the time when a few hundred soldiers could meet downtown late at night, take over the radio station, and announce that they are suspending certain political liberties for an indefinite period, promising to restore them later—once certain objectives have been accomplished. Today, a successful military coup would require the cooperation and mutual trust of twenty to thirty generals; keeping such a grand conspiracy under wraps would be extremely difficult. Moreover, some current Arab leaders came up through military coups of their own; they know what it takes to pull one off, so they are careful to put the appropriate safeguards in place. One example: Abbud al-Zumar, a leader of the Egyptian Jihad organization, was an Egyptian military intelligence colonel who came under increasing suspicion and had to leave the army.

The third path to power is the parliamentary path—and this medium will not work in the Arab world. No Arab leader will step down the way Gen. Wojciech Jaruzelski did in Poland, when he peacefully ceded power to Solidarity after it triumphed in popular elections. Arab regimes are more likely to maintain restricted political pluralism, in which the managers—not those who are managed—make the rules.

The fourth path is the popular uprising, which would also be very difficult to achieve in an Arab country. Such an uprising requires both a sharp socioeconomic crisis and a political crisis—including serious splits in the ranks of the core elite. Even if such an uprising were to occur, whoever prevailed among the competing factions of the elite would exercise brutal and indiscriminate repression of the populace, for fear of being overthrown by rivals.

The fifth path to power is what some are fond of calling "Islamization from below." They have this odd vision of Islamists building grassroots organizations in Arab countries, the citizenry flocking to these organizations, and the organizations growing to the point that the regimes are unable to ignore or quash them. Those who traffic in such ideas seem to be forgetting that, in order to form this sort of grassroots organization in an Arab country, you need the regime's permission—which of course would never be granted. They seem to be confusing most Arab regimes with Sweden.

In Egypt, Jordan, Algeria, Tunisia, and elsewhere, Islamists found the paths to power blocked. So they began to develop alternative means. Some Islamist groups sought ceasefires with the governing regimes, in part to deal with their own internal divisions. Other groups fled their home countries, relocating to less repressive settings. The latter switched their focus from the domestic to the global—and came up with a novel approach to attaining political power. Their goal was nothing less than humbling America, and they began to challenge various symbols of American power. They hoped to return to their own countries later, holding up a string of successful attacks against the superpower. They dreamed of bringing a message to existing Arab regimes: "Why are you afraid of America? America is a paper tiger. It could not even protect its most secure structures—not even the Pentagon." Can Islamist groups achieve their objectives through this kind of strategy? They certainly are trying.

5

Discussion

Robert B. Satloff, *The Washington Institute:* These two talks are provocative for numerous reasons, not least because both of you seem to conclude that regimes in the Middle East are not plagued by the same fear and vulnerability that we may feel in the United States regarding the Islamist threat. The issue is important because of the uncertainty in Washington concerning how this threat will—or will not—motivate local regimes to act in concert with our objectives.

The floor is now open to questions from the audience.

Kanan Makiya, *Iraq Research and Documentation Project:* Martin, in your address, why did you not include regime change in the Arab world at large—not just in Afghanistan—as one prong of a new, more decisive U.S. policy in the region? If the United States wants to send a message to the Arab world, should it not also have a target in the Arab world?

Martin Kramer: I do not think anyone wants to become involved in a war on two fronts simultaneously. First, achieve these two minimal goals in Afghanistan. Then America can look across the region, take the measure of other opportunities, and see what can be done to reverse—not just stall—this trend of growing contempt for the United States. There are other possibilities, but the United States will not be able to pursue other options until it has had clear success in the war that it has declared. First, there has to be something that looks and tastes like victory in Afghanistan.

Trudy Rubin, *Philadelphia Inquirer:* On Egypt, given that Sadatism continued after Anwar Sadat, will it continue after Hosni Mubarak? On Saudi Arabia, is there sufficient "rot" in the kingdom to cause problems, or is it containable?

Ibrahim Karawan: With regard to Egypt, I think one component of Sadatism would continue in a post-Mubarak era, regardless of Egypt's political configuration, and that is disengagement from the military component of the Arab-Israeli conflict. The strongest support for that disengagement comes from the most important institution in Egypt, the military establishment. The military are the first to appreciate the futility of going back to a situation of conflict. They know the gaps; they know the costs.

The second strongest support comes from the economic elites, who realize that engagement creates a bad climate for business and for economic issues. The third level of support—often underestimated—is that of the public. Some people think of the "Arab street" as those who appear at al-Azhar University shouting "Death to America," which, by the way, I believe they are entitled to do. The question is, do their opinions translate into official policy? This is the more serious matter.

In Egypt, support for disengagement is very strong and comes from the street. Only a few thousand individuals want to return to the struggle to liberate the land "from the river to the sea." This discussion is about those few thousand people. The rest of them do not want to send their kids to the Suez Canal again. Why should they? What happens to the political system in this scenario is a different story. You could have greater opening or greater restrictions, depending on who assumes power after Mubarak.

On Saudi Arabia, I do not think there is the kind of vulnerability to which some have referred. The regime uses multiple languages, and it is not completely without resources in the short run, contrary to some impressions. Sometimes people underestimate Saudi coping mechanisms.

Kramer: Many observers look at Saudi conduct since September 11 and assume that they are stonewalling because they do not want to confront the devil within. But the Saudis are not weak or afraid; they are ashamed. And there is a real difference. We saw the same kind of shame at work in the Egyptian government's investigation of the EgyptAir Flight 990 crash.

Currently, the Saudis are practicing what they do whenever they are ashamed, which is to engage in denial. When the Saudi interior minister asked U.S. officials, "Why are you focusing only on the Arabs that were on those airplanes? There were four hundred passengers," it is not because he is afraid. He is in denial over the shame of it. So we should be careful not to confuse issues and assume that every time America is stonewalled by its friends—Egyptians or Saudis— that those friends are actually shaking in their boots. They are not.

Karawan: You mentioned the source of Egyptian shame but did not explain it. Could you elaborate?

Kramer: There will be an article in the November 2001 *Atlantic Monthly** by a former pilot who investigated the EgyptAir affair; he went with the predisposition that perhaps the National Transportation Safety Board had made a mistake. But when he got to Egypt, he discovered a whole culture of denial that had arisen with deeply rooted cultural antipathy and resentment. He discovered that the other Egyptian pilots knew for certain that this plane was sentenced to the drink by the pilot. But the bureaucracy and the government were unable and unwilling to allow that an Egyptian national could have precipitated such a horrible event. This made the Egyptian investigation the mirror opposite of the American investigation.

The taking of collective responsibility for all Egyptian nationals is a curious thing. I am not suggesting that Western governments would not have done something similar. But in some Arab governments, you see this tendency to view the population as a herd of sheep tended by the shepherd. The collective shame that "one of the flock" could be responsible for a deed like this is simply overwhelming.

Philip Gordon, *Brookings Institution:* Even if America deals successfully with Osama bin Laden and Afghanistan, is there not great potential for the larger issue—that is, the nature of the regimes in Saudi Arabia and Egypt—to remain an American problem? Should we not think much more seriously about how to deal with that problem?

Kramer: The United States has first to decide what the meaning of September 11 is for the Middle East. Is it "day one" of an entirely

---

* William Langewiesche, "The Crash of EgyptAir 990," *Atlantic Monthly* 288, no. 4, pp. 41–52.

new era in which all past sins are forgiven and everyone is judged by their conduct henceforth? To some extent, that is the message the United States has sent in constructing its coalition. Lots of regimes have had their slates wiped clean. It seems that at this moment the only troublemaker who has carried a balance over into this new era is Iraq, although it is not at all clear just how much has been carried over. A decision will have to be made as to whether September 11 has created a new world in which everyone begins anew with a *tabula rasa*.

I am worried by the notion that the next phase, whether or not Iraq is a target, should involve American-initiated efforts to reform the politics of the Middle East, to create political space, and so forth. Right now, the United States does not have enough Arabic speakers to translate and analyze all of the plots fomenting against it; how will Washington reform the politics of the Arab world? It is a very tall order indeed.

A little humility is in order here. The United States, unlike Britain and France, has always been most effective when it operates "over the horizon" and "offshore." Those arguing for engagement in political reform are talking about a deep and intimate kind of involvement in an incredibly complex labyrinth.

The Arab world looks like a swamp, but it actually could be worse. When the Soviet Union collapsed, everyone assumed that things would get better in the Balkans. In much of Europe they did, but in that corner of Europe things got much worse. There has not been a Bosnia or a Rwanda in the Arab world in the last decade, and there has to be some caution in tinkering with the existing order. Yes, it would be wonderful if there were more space in the politics of the Arab world. But it would be disastrous if we had one or two or more Bosnias on our hands as a result.

Participant: Does the United States have a right to make certain demands of its coalition partners? What "litmus tests" should exist in the coalition-building phase of this campaign?

Karawan: Degrees of friendship are important to the formation of coalitions. But insisting that partner states must have a certain kind of political system in order to participate in a coalition is a luxury that no superpower can afford, especially in the post–September 11 environment. The United States may have a right to express its views about other political systems, but this does not mean that it can impose a "democratic test" for admission into its coalition; America would end up with very few partners if it did so.

Different types of cooperation are also important. For instance, some countries are willing to share their files on wanted terrorists, and others might view this as a modest contribution. Should it be deemed cowardly? No, such cooperation is useful at times when intelligence information is needed. Moreover, not all regimes are willing to make explicit verbal pronouncements about their particular contributions. Egypt happens to be among the countries whose level of security cooperation with the United States is quite extensive.

As the United States considers what course of action to take in the Middle East in the wake of September 11, it is important to remember the importance of context. Not that America should focus only on the motives of the terrorists—the United States could win over millions of Middle Easterners by legitimately addressing those grievances, but it would not appease the few thousand who support the terrorists.

The grievances of the Middle East are real, but it is crucial that legitimate expressions of Arab public opinion be separated from the supposed motives of the September 11 terrorists. Any concerted effort to link a particular Arab cause with the September 11 attacks would destroy any fruitful discourse about that cause. For example, although it is perfectly reasonable for Arab publics to be indignant concerning the Palestinian-Israeli conflict, it is pointless to speculate about whether the conflict's status might have played a role in encouraging or preventing the attacks on the United States. We should denounce such speculation, because any cause that gets associated—however tenuously—with September 11 is going to be weakened. Those who speculate in this manner have no real way of knowing what might have been. Theirs is a metaphysical argument.

Roger Harrison, *National Defense University:* I was raised in the tradition that took as an article of faith the adage "nations don't have friends, they have interests." Therefore, I take Dr. Kramer's point to have been that American and Israeli interests now and in the period ahead are coincident. Where might those interests not be coincident?

Kramer: Winning wars requires both myth-breaking and a true assessment of friendship. Friendship is, of course, based on the long-term confluence of interests and ideals. No one can tell me that the relationship between the United States and Britain is based solely on interests and has no element of friendship, which has to do with things that are shared beyond mere interests. The relationship between the United States and Israel falls in the same category, whether or not it is of the same order. Friends are those who, when the going gets tough, will stand by you, not just because your immediate interests are identical, but because there is some additional element like shared values, shared ideals, or a shared vision. There is probably a good deal of commonality among America's friends—not just Britain and Israel, but in Europe and elsewhere—who share these values.

Of course, I am not antagonistic to making Arabs and Muslims partners in the coalition against terrorism as well. But the United States should not rely on its Arab coalition partners for success in the Afghanistan campaign. The value of the coalition in the Middle East, as opposed to the coalition in southern Asia, is largely that of a totem; it is not an operational coalition. America needs a coalition with the Pakistanis, the Tajiks, and the Uzbeks in order to win the war in Afghanistan; but this grouping should not be confused with the totemic coalition in the Middle East. The greatest totem of them all, of course, is the insistence that America avoid making its campaign seem like a war between civilizations. That is a worthwhile goal, but it does not constitute an operational alliance.

Abdul Raouf al-Reedy, *former Egyptian ambassador to the United States:* How can America convince Arabs that it will now address the Arab-Israeli problem with more vigor? At the beginning of the Gulf War, President George H. W. Bush assured the region that after America liberated Kuwait, it would immediately turn its full attention to the Palestinian problem. A decade later, little real progress has been made. If the current administration offers a similar promise, will it follow through?

Karawan: The question is not whether the Arab-Israeli conflict should be addressed. It should be addressed on its own merits because it is a major source of instability in the region. But the same factors creating a stalemate before September 11 may still exist now, with no added reason to justify optimism other than the fact that it is better to try than not to try. It is important to realize that serious gaps remain between the Israelis and the Arabs, and that these gaps might now be wider, not narrower. This does not justify avoiding the issue, but neither should we predict a quick success in that effort unless America decides to vigorously twist Israel's arm, which I do not think will be the case.

Kramer: There is no doubt that bin Laden's public statements are fishing expeditions, and that he will use the Arab-Israeli issue to further his cause as others have. The difficulty is that solving these problems has become a much longer term proposition than many imagined. That is the lesson of the 1990s. Can you really afford to delay victory in the war against terrorism in order to solve these other long-term problems? There are phases in this war, and we should not confuse them or get them out of order. Issues like Iraq and Arab-Israeli relations will have to be addressed eventually; for now, let us stay focused on the present phase.

Mohammed Wahby, al-Mussawar *newspaper:* Was it really a feeling of contempt for the United States that motivated the September 11 attacks, or was it a sense of powerlessness among some extremist groups? Powerlessness is the opposite of contempt.

Kramer: I do not disagree with you. Yes, there is the sense of powerlessness. There is rage. There is hatred. But I argue that this mix becomes dangerous when you add to it contempt. For a potential recruit in a network like bin Laden's, the feeling of personal powerlessness can no doubt be a powerful motivation. Feelings of rage, hatred, and resentment are also very powerful. Yet, it is contempt that acts as a catalyst. And it is this contempt that can be most readily addressed because the United States has undeniable, overwhelming power.

That brings me to another point: what it means to have the upper hand. Basically, the United States has to create an aura of deterrence, to make people think not once, or twice, or ten times, but a thousand times before they contemplate acts like those of September 11. If America does not create that aura, it has come to the point of accepting terrorism as a way of life. This is the problem we have in Israel; terrorism is a way of life because we operate under so many constraints. But can America afford to accept terrorism as a way of life? If it cannot, then it will have to do something that Israel cannot do itself, which is to deliver an unrestrained blow to the perpetrators of these acts and those who shelter them. Frankly, the United States cannot allow itself to live as people in the Middle East do, with terrorism as a fact of life. It would be a betrayal of everything for which this country stands.

There has to be something that looks not like retribution (retribution is not part of American culture) but that nevertheless demonstrates the resolve of the United States and recreates the wall of deterrence. It is less important to rebuild the World Trade Center than it is to reerect that wall of deterrence.

American culture is a culture of "moving on." This is a country made of people who picked up, left everything behind, and moved on. Americans periodically reset the scoreboard. But the United States is now dealing with another kind of culture—one that keeps score. They have been keeping score since the Crusades, and the scoreboard is still running. This is the fundamental contradiction that America faces. Americans do not have to go back 600 years, but they do need to start keeping score, not so much for themselves, but for the sake of understanding how others perceive and feel about them. If there is a bottom line here, this is it: keep score. At this moment, it seems to me that the score is "Osama bin Laden three, the United States one."

PART THREE

Israel and the Palestinians, Post–September 11

6

Ehud Ya'ari

ISRAELI-PALESTINIAN RELATIONS have unfolded in a cyclical pattern: we reach a peace accord, we implement a ceasefire, the ceasefire breaks down, and we start all over again with new peace talks. This has been the basic cycle. The question is: will the horrible events of September 11 become a watershed in this Israeli-Palestinian dynamic? It may, but only once we reach Phase II—the post-Taliban era in Afghanistan. At present, the overall strategy—if we can call it that—of both Israel and the Palestinian Authority (PA) is "let's wait and see what comes next."

Coming into September 11, the intifada had been raging for a year, and it was problematic for both sides. From the Palestinian point of view, the uprising had failed to produce the expected dividends. Palestinian society, including the top echelon of its leadership, widely believed that the intifada was losing its way. In fact, every member of Yasir Arafat's immediate entourage—including all the military leaders and every security chief—objected to this policy as it was being pursued by the chairman.

I have always believed, and continue to believe, that the intifada is a long-term endeavor managed by Chairman Arafat from the time that he concluded the Oslo Accords with the Israeli government. People ask what Arafat is trying to achieve through the use of violence. Does he intend to move away from the peace process into a protracted confrontation with Israel? Or is he merely seeking to improve the terms of a possible deal ultimately reached through negotiations? I humbly submit to you that he wants both. On the one hand, from Arafat's point of view, the intifada is a long-term strategic choice, not merely a tactical move. On the other hand, a negotiated deal is possible in his thinking, as long as it does not preclude this long-term strategy. Arafat's vision involves maintaining constant tension between the two parties—sustaining fluctuating degrees of violence and perpetuating the ever-present possibility that violence will erupt.

Coming from the television trade, I am used to dealing with pictures. So please allow me to describe three scenes that will illustrate my point of view about the intifada. Scene One took place in 1994. Yasir Arafat, coming to the region for the first time since the Oslo Accords were signed, arrived at Rafah, on the border between Israel and Egypt. A young Israeli soldier said to a friend, "Gee, I didn't know Arafat was that tall." And why did Arafat seem so tall? Because, as he sat in his Mercedes, his *khaffiyah* scraped the roof of the car. No Israeli politicians or civilian officials were present, but the military looked into the matter and discovered the reason for Mr. Arafat's added height—an arch-terrorist named Jihad Amarin, whose name had been crossed off the list of Palestine Liberation Organization military personnel permitted to enter the country. Arafat was actually sitting on him. Moreover, crouched in the trunk of the car was another terrorist with a long track record, Mamduh Nofal, ex-military chief in Lebanon of the Democratic Front for the Liberation of Palestine. If I am not mistaken, three Kalashnikovs and some night-vision equipment were also stashed in the car. This is how Yasir Arafat came to Palestine, "in peace," for the first time. This was his entry, his curtain-raiser to the implementation of Oslo.

Scene Two again involves Mamduh Nofal, our friend riding in the trunk of the car with Arafat. Nofal later published a book serialized around the Arab world in nine newspapers. In the book, he wrote about the events of September 28, 2000—the day that Ariel Sharon, then an opposition leader, visited the Temple Mount—and he described what transpired that fateful evening. At this point, there were not yet any riots—no clashes, no bloodshed, no protest, no intifada. Nofal gives a detailed account of the instructions that Chairman Arafat personally issued to the Palestinian political and military leadership, and then in one-on-one meetings with the security chiefs; they were instructions for an intifada, to begin the next morning. I have since asked Nofal whether Arafat ever expressed any problem with his account of these events. He said, "No, no problem; they keep serializing the book." This description of how the intifada began tells us a great deal about who is responsible for it and about Arafat's ultimate control over what is going on today.

Scene Three took place at a meeting between Chairman Arafat and his top leadership, in which Arafat explained (and I am relying on very good sources), "We are not in a hurry for a Palestinian state. It does not have to happen in our generation—other generations are coming. We have time. We have to do our share, but not necessarily reach the objectives tomorrow morning." One of Arafat's men asked, "And what about the hundreds of casualties that the intifada has caused?" Arafat responded with a gesture, "They are all martyrs"—in Arabic, *kolohum shuhada.*

These three scenes demonstrate the fundamental elements of the chairman's operating framework. First, Arafat never really adopted the goal of peacemaking—not even immediately following Oslo. Second, Arafat was responsible for starting the intifada. Third, Arafat is not in a hurry for a Palestinian state; he can wait for another generation. These fundamental elements lay the groundwork for any post–September 11 adjustments.

Prior to September 11, Chairman Arafat had concluded that he should consider seeking an exit strategy from the intifada. It was a tough proposition, and he was not sure exactly how to carry it out. Nevertheless, there was every indication that he was beginning to move—or at least contemplate moving—in that direction, due to the problems he was having with the intifada.

One problem confronting Arafat was the absence of any real popular dimension to this uprising compared to the one that began in December 1987. The countryside, which was the backbone of the first intifada, has not played a role this time; neither have the 200,000 Arabs of Jerusalem. Likewise, the student body has hardly been engaged. By contrast, students led the first intifada—tens of thousands of young people in Gaza and the West Bank. Akram Hanieh—the man who, in my opinion, has the most influence on Arafat with respect to Israeli affairs—has written an article asking, "Where Are the Students?" Throughout the year, most students have been in class, preparing for exams; they have not been active in the uprising— other than the Hamas students, who have been busy trying to cook up explosives in the laboratory of al-Najah University in Nablus.

Moreover, the response of Arab nations to the Palestinian intifada has not been what the chairman had expected. For me, the great scene took place one morning when Egyptian president Hosni Mubarak appeared on the popular television program *Good Morning, Egypt.* As the two women were interviewing him, he interjected,

"You were asking me about a war." Although they had not been asking about any war, they replied, "Yes, Mr. President." And he said, "I am not going to let anyone fight to the last Egyptian soldier." On another occasion, in Qatar I believe, President Mubarak was asked why he was taking the liberty of telling the Palestinians what to do. He responded: "I am speaking on behalf of 50,000 graves of Egyptian soldiers who have given their lives for Palestine since 1948."

And finally, in general, international reaction to the intifada has been less than Yasir Arafat had hoped for. This is especially true of the U.S. position.

In light of these problems, Arafat made several adjustments after September 11. First, he was quick to declare himself to be on the side of the United States—only Prime Minister Tony Blair of England preceded him with a similar announcement. In his statement, Arafat assured U.S. officials that, whether or not a coalition was formed, he—Yasir Arafat—would stand behind the United States.

Second, the chairman has tried to activate a strategy of limited, partial exit from the intifada, working out a rough outline of this strategy with Israel's foreign minister, Shimon Peres. The new regime—his new form of confrontation—consists of a nominal ceasefire, but it leaves wide margins for the intifada to continue. This is a "ceasefire" with constant violations and fluctuating degrees of ongoing violence.

At the same time, the chairman has managed to work out a fairly successful ceasefire with Hamas, the main Palestinian Islamist movement. In this context, Arafat has supposedly threatened to outlaw terrorist organizations—but defining "terrorist" in the Palestinian lexicon is a real challenge. For their part, Hamas leaders and activists are making few statements about anything these days, including Arafat's threats.

And the chairman's latest post–September 11 adjustment has been an attempt to exercise greater control within his own jurisdiction. Before September 11, Arafat's modus operandi was something that I call a "willing suspension of control." Arafat willingly suspended his own control in order to allow a perception—a wrong perception—that he is not entirely in charge. He tried to convey the impression that irregulars—Tanzim, Fatah militia, Hamas, and the like (those supposedly outside of his control)—were producing all of the violence. Through this ruse, Arafat sought to allow the intifada to proceed without fully implicating himself.

But since September 11, the chairman has reached the conclusion that these tactics have, to a large degree, exhausted themselves, and that he must exercise a higher degree of control. It is not easy for Arafat to regain ground that he willingly lost. But he can do it, and he is doing it. One of the most telling anecdotes comes from the night that Arafat gave the instructions for the intifada to begin. According to Nofal's eye-witness account, one of Arafat's top military leaders advised, "Mr. President, we will be running the risk that Hamas takes the lead," to which Arafat apparently responded, "It doesn't matter who takes the lead." Of course, the chairman's point of view has evolved a bit since then.

Switching briefly to the Israeli side of the equation, the intifada has taught Israel a very important lesson concerning the priorities of Yasir Arafat, and it is a lesson that may have surprised many Israelis: Arafat's highest priority is not the establishment of a mini-Palestinian state in the immediate future. Indeed, Arafat and his people have begun to deride such a state as a "sovereign cage." We may have reached an ironic turning point now in which Israelis feel the urgency of establishing a Palestinian state—within the right contours and parameters—more than the Palestinians do, or at least more than their leader does.

All of us in Israel have come to understand that containment is the only viable option open to us, and that it is an option with serious limitations that has so far failed to produce most of the expected results—despite experiments with different forms and shades of this policy. Still, I do not believe Israel has the liberty to choose any other path at this moment. Indeed, vis-à-vis the intifada, there is no basic difference between the containment policy that former Prime Minister Ehud Barak pursued and the one that Prime Minister Ariel Sharon is currently executing—except, of course, for very distinct differences in rhetoric.

Along with containment, Israel is trying to gradually erode the staying power of the other side. In this regard, history gives us reason to be hopeful. If you go through the annals of the Israeli-Palestinian conflict, you will find that at no time were the Palestinians capable of maintaining a full-volume military confrontation for longer than a year or two. Within such a timeframe, their confrontational approach—first with the Jewish community and then with the state of Israel—always deteriorated. Either the Palestinians got into some form of civil war among themselves, or outside Arab powers intervened—politically or through military invasion, as in 1948.

So, this policy of containing the violence while trying to bring about an erosion of Palestinian staying power is Israel's only viable option. Many Israelis will tell you that we also have the alternative of unilateral separation: we just draw a line, build our defenses, and present the other party with a fait accompli. But this policy is not realistic; although it may be technically feasible, it is impossible from a political standpoint. Israel's few other options—going after Arafat or invading territory controlled by the Palestinian Authority—are far more risky than continuing the present containment policy.

Where does this leave us? Both the Israeli government and the Palestinian leadership believe—for different reasons—that maintaining some sort of controlled confrontation at the present level is less risky than attempting to change the rules of the game in any dramatic way. For its part, Israel has few alternatives, and maintaining the status quo is less risky than any of them. For his own reasons, Arafat also finds it in his interests to maintain the status quo.

As the two parties look toward the post-Taliban era, they are trying to predict how any Phase II in America's war on terror might affect them. They envision many possibilities—each of which raises intriguing questions. I will mention two areas that engender speculation. First, Israelis and Palestinians ponder what, if any, action the United States will take concerning terrorists in their own particular corner of the region. For example, Hizballah's chief of operations, Imad Mughniyeh, is now listed as one of the twenty-two terrorists most wanted by the United States—his name was presented in a press conference attended by President George W. Bush himself. What will this mean once Phase II begins? Will the United States go to Damascus, Beirut, and Tehran and present these leaderships with a request for Mughniyeh? And if these countries do not comply, what price will the United States exact?

Second, Israelis and Palestinians wonder what investment the United States will make in post-Taliban Afghanistan. Will the United States support the new regime and rebuild the country in any significant way? Under what conditions will it do so? And what lessons might Chairman Arafat derive from all this? These are questions the parties would like to have answered as they contemplate their future.

Let me conclude with a few remarks concerning that future. I do not believe a final status deal—resolving all outstanding issues between Israel and the Palestinians—was ever possible, nor do I believe it is possible now. Indeed, Arafat will not conclude a final peace agreement with Israel; this would not be consistent with his character. The chairman would tell you that he is better than Moses. Although Moses led his people to the promised land after forty years, he was stopped on Mount Nebo just on the other side of the Jordan River; from there, at best, he could see Jerusalem on a bright day. By contrast, over the course of the last forty years, Arafat brought his people to within mortar range of the walls of Jerusalem. Having come that close, he does not see himself as the man to sign a deal transferring legal ownership of any part of Palestine to the Jews. That is just not Arafat. If we want him to reach an agreement that includes compromises on basic issues, then we first have to transform him into a different Arafat.

If a final status deal is impossible, what, then, can we expect in the post-Taliban era? Assuming the Palestinians seek at least a partial exit from the intifada, then what is possible probably falls under the formula of "less for less." Israel will give the Palestinians less territory than Barak was willing to give; in exchange, Israel will receive from the Palestinians some sort of armistice that is short of a final status agreement. Although it would be less than a full peace agreement, such an armistice would be more than a simple ceasefire; it would include both territorial redeployment and commitment to an ongoing peace process. This armistice would be analogous to the ones concluded in 1948–49 between Israel and the Arab states.

In conclusion, if all goes well, the war in Afghanistan may have an effect similar to that of the Gulf War. The first intifada was slowly submerged into that war, and what emerged afterward was the Madrid peace conference. A similar situation may be developing now—with the best outcome being the kind of armistice agreement I just described. Many will consider this outcome unfortunate; I think, under the circumstances, that it may be good enough.

7

Khaled Abu Toameh

THE SEPTEMBER 11 ATTACKS came as Palestinians prepared to mark the first anniversary of the intifada—which had begun almost exactly one year earlier, on September 28, 2000. This was a very difficult period for Palestinians, because the intifada had concluded its first year with no obvious achievements. On the contrary, Yasir Arafat—and many Palestinians—felt that this uprising had taken us back fifteen or twenty years, destroying virtually everything built since Oslo. On top of the elements of self-destruction were added all of the Israeli measures taken against the Palestinians: the blockades, arrests, assassinations, incursions into Area A, bombings, F-16 attacks, and so on. Altogether, the situation on the ground was worse than ever.

In addition, many Palestinians, including Arafat, felt that they had become isolated in the international arena—no longer enjoying the sympathy and support even of the Arab world. Indeed, the Arab countries did nothing but talk; the only support they gave the Palestinians was rhetorical. Ehud described it very well in the context of Hosni Mubarak's remarks: Egypt will not fight for the Palestinians; it will not go to war for them. So, coming into September 11, the Palestinians felt that their Arab brethren had abandoned them. But they also felt that the Americans, the Europeans, and the rest of the world were no longer sympathetic to the Palestinian cause. The leaders of these countries were asking, "What do you want? Ehud Barak offered you almost everything, and you turned him down. You have nothing to complain about. You are responsible for Sharon coming to power, and you deserve Sharon."

Another important problem confronting the Palestinian Authority (PA) on the eve of September 11 was the destruction of the Palestinian economy. Many of the PA's institutions were bankrupt; many were forced to close down. Yasir Arafat was unable to pay the salaries of most workers, including the police force. One reason for this dire economic situation was that many Arab countries were not fulfilling their promises to support the intifada financially. The one country that did supply funds to the Palestinians was Iraq. Indeed, Saddam Husayn's men were very active in the West Bank and Gaza, visiting the homes of Palestinian martyrs and offering $10,000 to each family. Saddam's men are continuing to make these payoffs today, while Yasir Arafat offers only $1,000 or $2,000 to these families—that is all he can afford.

So, the period leading up to the September 11 attacks was a difficult one for the Palestinians. Once the attacks occurred, there were several initial Palestinian reactions: the street reaction, the official reaction, and the official reaction to the street reaction.

Within three or four hours after news of the attacks began coming out of Washington, Yasir Arafat called an emergency meeting in Gaza of his advisors and the heads of his security forces. One of those who participated in that meeting described it to me. "It seems that Uncle Sam has been beaten severely," Arafat told his advisors. He asked them for their interpretation of events. One of the security force heads said, "Don't worry. It will turn out to be another Timothy McVeigh." Another advisor offered, "I'm sure it's the Red Army." Arafat asked, "What do you mean, the Red Army?" The man answered, "Look, the Japanese have an account to settle with the Americans."

At that point, Arafat asked his men, "What if it turns out to be a Palestinian?" All of his advisors were in agreement, "No problem. We will say it was Hamas, or Islamic Jihad. We can always throw responsibility on the Islamists." Then Arafat asked, "But what if they say that I am harboring these people and not arresting them?" His advisors responded again, "No problem. We will crack down on them as we did back in 1996, following American pressure after the suicide bombings."

Toward the end of the meeting, some of Arafat's advisors came into the room and announced, "President Arafat, there are pictures of Palestinians celebrating in the streets. This is causing us a lot of damage and embarrassment." Arafat asked, "Where? Who?" Arafat's men responded, "In Jerusalem, Ramallah, and Nablus, Palestinians have been celebrating the attacks and supporting Osama bin Laden." Arafat looked at Jabril Rajoub, who was sitting next to him, and said: "Stop them. Give me Ghazi Jabali," commander of the Palestinian police. Arafat picked up the phone and said, "Ghazi, no more demonstrations. Anyone who demonstrates goes to prison."

I am one of the Palestinian journalists who was out in the street that day. I had a crew with me. Palestinians were honking their horns, flashing "V" for victory signs, and handing out baklava and kanafi, traditional Arab sweets. I asked, "What are you celebrating?" and they answered, "Didn't you hear? America has been destroyed. The White House has been destroyed, and the Pentagon. Bush is hiding. America has been destroyed. Next, Israel is going to be destroyed." That was the mood in the street. I prepared a videotape reporting the situation and submitted it.

A few hours after Arafat's meeting with the heads of his security forces, several Palestinian journalists and television producers—myself included—each received a telephone call. A senior PA official, whom I do not want to name, was on the other end of the line: "The president orders you not to cooperate in tarnishing the image of the Palestinian people." I said, "Excuse me, what does that mean?" He said, "No more filming of celebrations, because that plays into the hands of our enemies. They would use it against us, and that would be harmful to the higher national interest of the Palestinian people." I told him, "Look, I am a journalist. I don't know what you are talking about. If there are celebrations, that's your problem." He said, "Yes. It is our problem, and we are trying to stop it. But because East Jerusalem is not under our control, we rely on you, Palestinian journalists, not to collaborate with these foreign crews who are trying to distort the image of the Palestinian people." I asked him what would happen next. He said, "Look, we are already dealing with journalists who are involved in this; you can call some of your colleagues in Ramallah and Gaza and ask them what can happen to them if they dare to collaborate with the foreign crews." And that was the end of the conversation.

From this point on, the PA's policy was to try to contain the damage that had been done to the Palestinian public image, as they saw it. Arafat immediately instructed Hanan Ashrawi to step in and try to save the Palestinians' reputation. Ashrawi organized a candlelighting event outside the American consulate; the PA notified journalists and tried to make sure that as many of us as possible covered this event. Then, we had the blood donation in Gaza by Arafat himself, and again the PA made every effort to get journalists to come.

So Arafat's earliest response to the September 11 attacks was to try to erase the impression that Palestinians were celebrating; instead, he tried to portray Palestinians as sympathizing with the Americans. Next, Arafat and the PA started thinking more generally about how to relate to the events surrounding September 11—this enormous turning point in world politics. They tried to determine how they themselves fit into the new coalition. Arafat immediately decided that the Palestinians must join. "We have no other choice," he reasoned, "because we also are victims of terrorism; we are the victims of Israel's terrorism—and Israel's terrorism is no different than the terrorism used against the West." This is the official Palestinian line. Even today, Palestinian officials are declaring that any coalition against terrorism should address Israeli "terrorism"—namely the bombings, assassinations, blockades, and purported starvation of the Palestinian people.

In responding as he did to the September 11 attacks, Arafat's goal was to avoid repeating the mistake he had made during the Gulf War when he sided with Saddam Husayn. According to those around him, Arafat learned a lesson then. Today, the Palestinian street still remains much more radical than the PA—or at least the PA's official posture. But this time, Arafat was not prepared to allow the Palestinian street to drag him toward extremism. He was not prepared to fall into that trap again.

Having associated themselves with the U.S.-led coalition against terrorism, the Palestinians are now waiting to reap the fruits of this "new world order" as they see it. They hope to be rewarded at the end of this war as they were rewarded after the Gulf War—which brought about the Madrid conference and, later, Oslo. The Palestinians reason that if they behave themselves in this new war in Afghanistan—if they sit on the sidelines and do not make trouble for the Americans or anyone else—then, when the war is over, they will be rewarded for having been on the "right side."

Now, it is a waiting game for the PA, which is putting all of its hopes on the West, and on America in particular. Although the war in Afghanistan is not yet over, those in the Palestinian leadership already see positive developments resulting from their choice: the Americans are floating a new peace initiative, and Yasir Arafat is once again a welcome leader in London and other Western capitals. Arafat is determined not to destroy these achievements; indeed, the chairman wants to be received at the White House as well.

So, although on the eve of September 11, Arafat found himself in isolation, he is once again returning to the stage. As he sees it, the September 11 attacks have actually helped him to reemerge, because he has chosen the right side this time. He wants to be seen in league with the "good guys," fighting the "bad guys." As for Osama bin Laden—who cares? For the first time, Palestinian officials are employing all kinds of negative phrases against him—they do not appreciate his using the Palestinian cause in his speeches. Palestinians are saying, "Keep us out of this. We are not involved."

Arafat is prepared to wait. He is even prepared to make deals with Shimon Peres, whom he greatly admires and appreciates. If Peres asks for a ceasefire, and the Americans support it, Arafat will agree to a ceasefire. But he is not prepared to stop the intifada. Even when the recent ceasefire announcement was made, Palestinian officials, with the help of the Palestinian media, declared, "We have a ceasefire, but the intifada will continue." In other words, the PA is explicitly calling for a prolongation of the armed struggle.

What Arafat wants is an intifada on a low burner; he does not want a wide-scale military engagement. It is fine to have a number of drive-by shootings here and there, sporadic incidents of stone throwing, flare-ups of popular resistance, and similar occurrences. However, Arafat does not want an all-out confrontation at this time.

Moreover, Arafat has instructed the Palestinian police to stay out of the confrontation. That is why, as an organized force, they have not been officially involved. I am not suggesting that Arafat controls all of the police; if this intifada has done anything, it has caused many Palestinian policemen to break ranks. In the morning, you see a Palestinian policeman directing traffic in downtown Ramallah. At night, that same policeman, without a uniform, takes a gun from the refugee camp where he lives and carries out an attack. Of course, he does not do it with his own AK-47, because the weapon could be traced. Still, there are not fifteen, or even fifty, Palestinian policemen standing there shooting—contrary to what many believe. Rather, groups of Fatah, Hamas, Popular Front for the Liberation of Palestine, or Democratic Front for the Liberation of Palestine activists are primarily responsible for carrying out the attacks—but they sometimes do so with the help of these dissident Palestinian policemen.

As for Hamas, many believe that the intifada has caused this organization to become much more popular among Palestinians. In fact, some public opinion polls show a rise in support for Hamas in the West Bank and, especially, in Gaza. Support has also increased for the suicide attacks that Hamas has carried out; the Palestinian street sees these attacks as being effective and successful. A Hamas suicide bomber who is capable of killing twenty or twenty-five Israelis is considered a hero, and is glorified as a *shahid* (martyr) in the official Palestinian media. The Palestinian youth—even the children—are encouraged to follow in the footsteps of these heroes. The irony is that Arafat's own media encourages the Palestinian people to emulate the suicide bombers. He is driving his people into the arms of Hamas and Islamic Jihad by glorifying their deeds and acts. But in doing so, he is undermining his own regime.

So what has Hamas's position been since September 11? Their official line is, "We are against terrorism, especially terrorism directed against innocent civilians. Of course, the American people are a friendly people; they are innocent. Therefore, we condemn these attacks—despite our disagreements with the Bush administration and other U.S. administrations concerning their bias toward Israel."

Essentially, Hamas is trying to draw a line between the American people and the U.S. administration. The group is hoping that the American people will start asking questions about why the attacks happened, and that Americans will call for a review of U.S. policy toward Israel. Hamas, and many other Palestinians, are also attempting to use the September 11 attacks to drive a wedge between America and Israel. Their message to the American people is, "This is all happening to you because of your unwavering support for Israel. It is happening because you give Israel so many weapons, and Israel uses these weapons against our people. It is time for you to revise your policy. It is time for you to pressure your own government to change."

Indeed, since September 11, there has not been one Hamas or Islamic Jihad suicide bombing inside Israel. Suicide bombings have been carried out, but not by either of these groups. Hamas's current policy is to halt the suicide operations because the organization would have no way to explain them to the West—and to the United States in particular. Launching suicide bombings now, only weeks after the attacks in New York and Washington, would tempt the United States to identify Hamas as a terrorist group, much like Osama bin Laden's al-Qaeda. Hamas is trying, instead, to project the image of a nationalist movement with its own agenda, seeking to liberate its homeland. Thus, Hamas and the PA are taking the same basic attitude toward the September 11 bombings. They are trying to stay clear and see what they can get out of this whole tragedy.

We could talk for hours about Yasir Arafat's "strategy," but none of those close to him really know where he is leading his people. In reality, he is behaving in a reflexive manner more than pursuing a strategy. One gets the impression—in speaking with those who talk to him every day—that Arafat wakes up in the morning and asks what is going on. If the wind is blowing in this direction, he goes this way. If the wind is blowing in another direction, he goes that way. If he is being pressured to condemn bin Laden, he condemns him. If he is forced to crack down on Hamas, he cracks down on Hamas. But tomorrow, if he is no longer required to keep a Hamas leader in prison, he will release him. It is very spontaneous. To conclude, I believe that Yasir Arafat's only strategy is keeping himself in power as long as possible.

8

Flynt Leverett*

THE BUSH ADMINISTRATION laid out the framework of its policy in the Israeli-Palestinian arena well in advance of September 11. The administration endorsed the Mitchell Commission's report in May 2001 and adopted the commission's recommendations as the basis for administration policy. In June 2001, the director of central intelligence, George Tenet, went to the region and brokered a security work plan to help us carry out the first phase of the Mitchell program—the cessation of violence—and to set us on a course of confidence-building measures.

Those two linked elements, the Mitchell report and the Tenet security work plan, remain the framework of U.S. policy. As we implement this policy, we hope, first of all, to reduce and eliminate the ongoing violence between Israelis and Palestinians. We want to diminish and eradicate the violence—in return for Palestinian security options. We would like to work with the Israelis to take steps to improve the day-to-day lives of Palestinians in the West Bank and Gaza. We would then like the two sides to implement reciprocal confidence-building measures to restore some measure of trust between them. Hopefully, increased trust will lead to a renewed political process that will focus on implementing agreements that Israel and the Palestinians already have signed; of course, the political process will also focus, ultimately, on final status issues.

The basic thrust of U.S. policy still holds after September 11. The one new wrinkle is the president's endorsement of Palestinian statehood—which he gave on October 3, 2001. As the president himself pointed out in his remarks, the vision of an ultimate settlement has included the idea of a Palestinian state for quite some time. But the president carefully conditioned his endorsement to make it clear that creating a Palestinian state cannot, in any way, jeopardize the

---

*Mr. Leverett's remarks represent his own views and not those of the State Department, the Central Intelligence Agency, or the United States government.

security of the state of Israel. The Sharon government itself is now on record as accepting the idea of a Palestinian state—obviously, under certain conditions.

So the basic tenets of U.S. policy remain unchanged after September 11. We still seek a just, lasting, and comprehensive peace between Israel and the Palestinians—indeed between Israel and all Arab states. At the same time, we want to ensure Israel's security and its qualitative edge.

Now that I have briefly described the framework of the Bush administration's policy regarding Israel and the Palestinians, I will respond to the observations of the two previous speakers. They focused on the impact of the events of September 11 (and of U.S. efforts to put together a counterterrorism coalition) on both sides. Of course, Israel was a partner of the United States in the fight against international terrorism well before September 11. Indeed, America has benefited from close security and intelligence cooperation with Israel for many years. From the perspective of my former position as a Central Intelligence Agency analyst, I can personally testify to the value and intensity of that relationship. Those links—security and intelligence cooperation—are even more valuable to us now; they are ongoing and, if anything, intensifying in the aftermath of September 11.

A lot has been said about Phase I and Phase II of the U.S. campaign against terrorism. Everyone understands that, at this point in the campaign, we are giving operational priority to Osama bin Laden and to groups affiliated with his al-Qaeda network. This is a reasonable approach, given that bin Laden and his affiliates were responsible for the deaths of thousands on American soil on September 11, as well as many others in previous terrorist incidents. If we succeed in Phase I of this campaign, it will benefit not just the United States, but all free nations, including the state of Israel.

We also have a longer-term goal in this campaign, which the president has stated very clearly. Our ultimate goal is to eliminate all terrorism of "global reach." That rubric clearly encompasses terrorist activity of the sort that has been aimed against Israel and Israelis. No one gets a pass on this.

There has been a lot of uncertainty, even anxiety, about the way the United States has gone about putting together its antiterrorism coalition. But the U.S. effort to build an antiterrorism coalition must be seen in the context of the president's larger goal of eliminating all terrorism of global reach. There is no double standard; all terror is bad. Terrorism directed against non-Americans is just as significant as terrorism directed against Americans. Terrorism committed by groups that are not—as far as we know—affiliated with Osama bin Laden is just as reprehensible as terrorism committed by those who are linked to bin Laden. As I said, though, our current operational priority is to go after bin Laden and the al-Qaeda network.

In the course of prosecuting this campaign, we are engaging in discussions with countries that we have previously designated as state sponsors of terrorism. We are doing so, first of all, for tactical benefit. If these regimes are in a position to offer information that will enable us to prosecute Phase I of our campaign more effectively—and perhaps with less risk to U.S. military personnel—we would be foolish not to avail ourselves of that information. That being said, we have no illusions about the track record of the countries we have designated as state sponsors. We have not forgotten why they were designated as such in the first place. But our engagement with some of these regimes has a broader strategic objective at this point—to serve the president's ultimate goal of eliminating all terrorism of global reach.

These countries now have an opportunity to move in the right direction—to move away from a past that warranted their designation as state sponsors. By helping us in the campaign against al-Qaeda, some of these states may be taking a first step in that direction. And quite frankly, September 11 gives us a certain amount of leverage with them. A number of these regimes are concerned right now; they do not want to get on the wrong side of the United States in this counterterrorism campaign, and it is strategically worthwhile for us to explore just how far we can get them to go in the right direction. We will not lower the standards we apply in deciding whether to remove a country from the state sponsors list. But without giving anyone a pass, we can still take advantage of this strategic opportunity.

We are not excluding Israel from this coalition. And we are not in any way building this coalition on Israel's back. Significantly, as we continue to develop U.S. policy, the president's larger goal—of eliminating all terrorism of global reach—is very much part of our planning and daily frame of reference.

With regard to the Palestinians, I certainly agree with Ehud Ya'ari that Yasir Arafat and other senior leaders in the Palestinian Authority (PA) did not want to repeat the mistake they made during the Gulf War—when they sided with Saddam Husayn and found themselves on the wrong side of the United States and most of the rest of the world. In the aftermath of September 11, senior PA officials, including Arafat, made multiple public condemnations of the attacks. They have also rejected Osama bin Laden's attempts to appropriate the Palestinian cause as his own. More concretely, at our request, the PA has taken steps to block financial transactions by terrorist individuals and groups named in Executive Order 13224 issued on September 24, 2001. The PA is in the process of establishing a permanent office to track money laundering and to monitor illicit financial flows through Palestinian banks; this will be important in implementing the executive order.

I also agree with Mr. Ya'ari that Arafat is looking for an exit package—for a way to get started down the road laid out in the Mitchell-Tenet framework. Since the beginning of the current intifada, we have seen three kinds of anti-Israel violence. First, Palestinian crowds have come into violent conflict with Israeli security forces. Second, Hamas, Islamic Jihad, and other rejectionist groups outside the PA framework have initiated violence. And third, of course, elements of the Palestinian security services themselves—along with other elements of the PA and Palestine Liberation Organization apparatus—have perpetrated violence.

I think it is fair to say that since September 11, we have seen Arafat do more against all three of these types of violence than we have seen him do previously. He is not doing enough—on a sufficiently sustained basis—to allow us get onto the Tenet-Mitchell track. He must do more. Nevertheless, I essentially agree that Arafat has shown greater interest in getting onto a more constructive road—particularly since September 11.

I was also struck by Mr. Ya'ari's comments that right now, and for the foreseeable future, containment—as he described it—is the only sustainable strategy for Israel. I understand much of the logic in that statement, and I may agree with large portions of that logic. One part of the conclusion, though, makes me uncomfortable—that Palestinian public opinion in the West Bank and Gaza is radicalizing. A systematic review of recent polls conducted in Palestinian areas would confirm this development, which makes it all the more urgent for the PA to take steps on the security front that will allow us get started on the Tenet-Mitchell track.

Also, it is imperative for the United States—working with the Israelis—to pick up on any opportunity that presents itself to get the process moving forward. I am a bit uncomfortable with the idea of having to wait years before seeing any progress. I fully appreciate the difficulties in going down the road laid out in Tenet-Mitchell and have no illusions that it will be either quick or easy—even once we get started. But we have to get moving; if not, the evolution of popular opinion, particularly in the territories, will be working against us.

Ami Ayalon has described the counterterrorism coalition that took shape during the time he was director of the Israel Security Agency. That coalition did, indeed, include a number of outside players, such as Egyptians, Jordanians, and some of my colleagues from the U.S. intelligence community. But the heart of that coalition was robust counterterrorism cooperation between the Israeli security services and their Palestinian counterparts.

In the long run, the interests of both parties—and the interests of Israeli security—are best served by getting us moving down the path toward a negotiated settlement. As frustrating as our experiences in the recent past have been, this remains the only truly viable and sustainable option open to the parties. The Bush administration continues to be deeply interested in working with the parties to get everyone moving on that track.

9

Discussion

Robert B. Satloff, *The Washington Institute:* Flynt, you discussed the leverage that the United States has had since September 11 with states on the terrorism list. Nevertheless, we continue to see considerable terrorist activity in the region. This activity includes actions by Hizballah over the border; actions by Hamas in Alei Sinai; an attempted car bombing by Islamic Jihad in Jerusalem; and the murder of Rehavam Ze'evi, Israel's minister of tourism, by the Popular Front for the Liberation of Palestine (PFLP). One thing connects the organizations involved in all four of these attacks: Damascus. Someone is clearly testing what kind of leverage the United States has after September 11. And I would suggest that whatever leverage we may have had has pretty much withered away—at least in the eyes of those doing the testing. We certainly have not sent the signal that we are exercising that leverage.

Flynt Leverett: As far as dealing with some of the states we have designated as sponsors of terrorism, I do not think our leverage has dissipated. We are just beginning to apply that leverage and see how far it goes. Barely a month has passed since September 11; with some of these states, we have just begun our dialogue on counterterrorism issues. Believe me, with regard to all of the incidents that you named— particularly the involvement of the PFLP in the assassination of the Israeli minister of tourism—we are weighing in very heavily with Damascus. We are making sure that the Syrian regime understands how it will be hurt if it continues to maintain links to groups that engage in these kinds of activities. As I say, we want to see just how far we can go with that kind of engagement, but we are really at the beginning.

Dennis B. Ross, *The Washington Institute:* Ehud, I would like to agree with your conclusion, although I disagree with your analysis. You seem to think that Yasir Arafat is reacting on a day-by-day basis, depending on the mood, not making a choice unless he has to. When he went to Oslo, it was, in a sense, because he had no choice. If we are to move down this path again, we must agree to give Arafat absolutely no choice in the matter. We must leave him no choice but to negotiate.

Ehud Ya'ari: This is the old argument. My response is that Arafat does have a strategy, and he is very disciplined about it. The strategy for him is to get onto the land—whatever he can get—without burying the conflict. Arafat does not want to become the undertaker of what he perceives as basic Palestinian rights.

Joseph Sisco, *Sisco Associates:* The press has given indications that the United States might put forward a substantive proposal. Could you comment on when a substantive American proposal might be feasible—and when it might be desirable?

Leverett: I cannot give you a concrete answer as to when the administration might move forward with a major public statement. We are constantly reviewing the situation; if we reach a point at which we think a statement would be helpful, we will make one. As of now, we have made no decisions on a major administration statement.

The U.S. initiative is already on the table—the Tenet-Mitchell plan. As I discussed earlier, this plan envisions eventually restarting the political process; the political process will focus on further implementing agreements that the parties have already signed, and it will ultimately deal with final status issues. If the U.S. government were to make a major policy statement at this point, I anticipate that it would be within the Tenet-Mitchell framework. I do not expect any new or separate initiative.

Ya'ari: The best kind of U.S. proposal would be an adaptation of the original invitation to Madrid—nothing beyond that.

Michael Stein, *The Washington Institute:* We all know that at the end of the road, there is going to be a Palestinian state. At a Washington

Institute event in 1998, Ariel Sharon sat on a platform with Abu Ala, speaker of the Palestinian parliament, and made that very statement. But the devil is in the details—and the details are enormously complicated and difficult. As a loyal American, I think it was a big mistake for President Bush to come out and endorse Palestinian statehood on October 3, 2001. The endorsement looks like a benefit accruing from the September 11 attacks and a pay-off to other parties in order to bring them into the coalition. It was an American policy error.

It seems to me that our policy, as we articulate it, is often based on platitudes and self-deception. I hear words that sound good but have no real meaning in light of the conditions on the ground—conditions that our first two speakers described very well. For example, we always use the term "just peace," but the term is never defined; it cannot be defined—because "just" means different things to different people. Without a definition of "just peace," how can a policy based on a "just peace" have any real meaning?

Similarly, we talk about "comprehensive peace"—yet we already know that there are too many complicated issues to allow for a solution on a comprehensive basis. Moreover, we have already seen that Arafat cannot sign an agreement that ends the conflict and the Palestinian claim. So what does "comprehensive" mean?

We should stop using these sound-good platitudes. We should stop fooling ourselves that all the issues can be solved "comprehensively"—all at once, and "justly"—in a way that can meet everyone's definition of "just." Instead, we should deal with the issues on their individual merits.

Leverett: First, we have not substantively modified our approach to the Israeli-Palestinian conflict as a result of the events of September 11. We have tried to make that clear—perhaps your question indicates that we need to work at it harder. The basic framework of our approach to improving the situation between Israel and the Palestinians, and our basic position regarding Palestinian statehood, were laid out well before September 11.

You may question the president's timing, but the endorsement of Palestinian statehood was not linked to the events of September 11. We have tried to make that clear—in the way that we have dealt with Israel since September 11, and in the way that we have put the coalition together.

Second, you ask what the phrase "just peace" means. At a minimum, it means two states—an Israeli state and a Palestinian state—so that Israelis can be secure within their boundaries and Palestinians can determine their own political future. I cannot tell you what the exact borders of those two states should be. I cannot set out an arrangement for Jerusalem or for how refugees should be handled. These are final status issues that have to be worked out between the parties. But I can tell you that, in the end, a "just peace" is going to mean two states.

I also want to take issue, respectfully, with your point about "comprehensive peace." When we say that a peace must ultimately be comprehensive, we do not mean that it has to be reached all at once. In fact, I see real risks in trying to do too much at once in negotiations, and I am not trying to advocate that course for Israeli-Palestinian negotiations. Arriving at a "comprehensive peace" in which all of the difficult issues have been dealt with certainly will take a long time. But at the end of the day—however long that day—this is our goal.

Janine Zacharia, Jerusalem Post: Mr. Leverett, you and other Bush administration officials seem to suggest that this is a comprehensive war on terrorism. You assure the Israelis that you will not abide any attempt to distinguish between "bad" terrorism and "good" terrorism—and you affirm that the war on terrorism will indeed go on to Phase II. But administration officials add a caveat; they say that in Phase II, we are going to go after terrorism with "global reach." That seems to suggest a somewhat limited war on terrorism. So my question is: does the Bush administration consider Hamas, Palestinian Islamic Jihad, and groups of that nature to be terrorists of global reach?

Leverett: Yes. I certainly believe that groups like Hizballah and Hamas would meet the definition of terrorist groups with global reach.

Satloff: Thank you—a very important clarification.

Charles Krauthammer, *Washington Post Writers Group:* Ehud, you said that Israel's only alternative is a policy of containment—living with terrorism as a way of life. I am not sure Israelis can tolerate that. Looking at the polls, one gets the impression that a significant number of Israeli citizens prefer another option, that is to attack, destroy, and expel the Palestinian Authority (PA). In your view, is that a viable alternative?

Ya'ari: Containment is our only option now. Basically, the decision as to whether we switch gears and embark on a campaign we do not want to undertake is not ours to make. It is up to Arafat—just as it was in Lebanon, in Jordan, and in other places.

Hopefully, containment will lead to some sort of an armistice—probably the sort of "less for less" arrangement I described earlier in which Israel gives less and receives less in return. If the parties cannot reach an armistice, Israel may find itself in a situation in which it must take a different posture vis-à-vis Arafat—against its better judgment and probably against its interests. That is possible.

David Makovsky, *The Washington Institute:* I question the assumption that Arab countries—particularly Egypt—might get Arafat to do something that he does not want to do. We have not seen significant Arab influence in seven years, perhaps since 1994 with the Gaza-Jericho agreement. For instance, there is an assumption that Egyptian president Hosni Mubarak influences Arafat; Mubarak may have the capability, but he has not shown the motivation.

Barbi Weinberg, *The Washington Institute:* Throughout the period in which this peace process was supposedly unfolding, massive anti-Israel propaganda continued to be spread among the Palestinian people. This included the indoctrination of children in the Palestinian school system. If the parties do resume a peace process, how will the propaganda problem be handled?

Leverett: You raise an excellent point about the trends in Palestinian public opinion. Something like this is always a very complicated phenomenon—many factors contribute to it. Look at Gaza, for example:

a million Palestinians live there; half of them are under the age of eighteen and have virtually no economic prospects. That is an environment ripe for these kinds of developments. Nevertheless, I think you are exactly right. Incitement is a critical problem. If we are going to get out of the mess that we are in now, we must deal with the Palestinians on this issue.

Khaled Abu Toameh: Sometimes I listen to American policymakers and wonder if they really know what is happening on the Palestinian side. (Applause.) They talk to Arafat and Nabil Sha'ath and Abu Ala, and seem to ignore the Palestinian street. Is this because the U.S. administration is naive? Does the administration see what is happening on the ground?

As long as the United States continues to support these very corrupt regimes, the Palestinian street will go in one direction while the regime goes in another. That is exactly what is happening now. Before September 11, Arafat had been telling his people that the United States is an enemy. Just a few weeks before the World Trade Center attacks, Arafat ordered his mufti to utter a special prayer asking God to destroy America and Britain. Today, Arafat cannot control his people—the very people he has been inciting. And now, the Palestinian street is much more radical than the PA; the Palestinian street supports Osama bin Laden. It is time for the State Department to hire Arab translators, or to send people out into the field to see what is happening. (Applause.)

Leverett: I accept your point that we need more people trained in the Arabic language and local dialects—those who can really take the pulse of Arab society. I say this as something of an Arabist myself.

However, I do not quite understand what you would have us do in terms of engaging with someone other than Arafat. I have considered the other various figures within the Palestinian community who have a chance of commanding considerable popular allegiance. It seems to me that those individuals would be inimical to both Israeli and U.S. interests. Whatever problems or dissatisfactions we may have with the PA, the alternatives are far more disturbing and threatening. With whom would you have us engage?

Satloff: You raise a very important question, which gives me the perfect opportunity to recommend a Washington Institute publication to which Khaled and Ehud both contributed: *After Arafat? The Future of Palestinian Politics* (The Washington Institute, 2001). This study explores the very topic you raise.

PART FOUR

Is Democracy the Answer? Principles and Interests in U.S. Middle East Policy

10

Kanan Makiya

ADDRESSING THE CULTURAL AND HISTORICAL REASONS for the lack of democracy in the Arab world is more important than ever in the wake of September 11. Such broad issues cannot be covered adequately in this forum, though, and attempting to do so would divert us from a more pressing question: given the events of September 11, should the United States make democracy promotion a higher priority in its dealings with Arab states? The answer is "yes," and what remains is to assess the enormous challenge that such an undertaking represents for the United States. For that purpose, I will focus on two countries: Saudi Arabia, America's closest Arab ally, and Iraq, which is still the best place to launch a new U.S. policy of facilitating fundamental regime change in a democratic direction, despite all that has happened since the Gulf War.

Before discussing these examples, it is important to make note of an unfortunate misperception that has grown since September 11. We must keep in mind that those attacks were conceived and executed by Arabs, not by Afghans, Pakistanis, or Muslims in general. Arabs constitute less than 20 percent of the world's Muslim population, yet some would tar the whole Muslim world with the problems of its Arab component. Recently, television programs have been showing more than a few images of Afghan or Pakistani students allegedly studying the Qur'an, or of Osama bin Laden looking like the prophet Muhammad in his cave. When such images are juxtaposed with those of planes flying into the World Trade Center, or of all the human suffering caused by that cataclysmic event, a powerful association is established between Islam and terrorism, one that no amount of well-intentioned explanation may be able to dispel. That association is wrong and, from a political standpoint, very troubling. In fact, the recently initiated bombing of Afghanistan may have led America somewhat astray from what should be the real focus of the war on terrorism.

Offering harsh criticism of the Middle East has never been easy for me, even when it is well deserved. I have always written as a person committed to that region—a person who holds the land and religion of his birth in very high regard, however secular he himself may be. Thus, I find it difficult to admit that a certain rot has taken hold in the Arab Middle East, and that this rot is responsible for the single greatest atrocity in American history.

Even the non-Arab Taliban are a symptom of this rot. As others have pointed out, the Taliban are a creation of Pakistani president Pervez Musharraf's intelligence services. Yet, they have also been financed by Saudi oil wealth, even after their years of struggle against Russian occupation. The Taliban have nothing to do with Afghan history or traditions; they practice an extreme version of Wahhabism, a retrograde sect of Islam that is obsessed with purity. This sect views both non-Muslims and non-Wahhabi Muslims as a form of pollution on the entire "Land of Muhammad," which is the phrase that bin Laden used when talking about the presence of U.S. troops in Saudi Arabia. Wahhabism takes its name from the eighteenth-century fanatical reformer Muhammad ibn Abd al-Wahhab, who allied himself with those tribal warlords who eventually became the Saudi dynasty. Thus, the full blame for the emergence of the Taliban cannot be laid on Pakistan; Wahhabism was nonexistent in that area until very recently.

Osama bin Laden grew up on Wahhabism, which is still taught in Saudi schools, and he turned it against the Saudi rulers when they violated its principles during the Gulf War. Yet, it is only through the oil wealth and power of this regime—long an ally of the United States—that Wahhabism has been able to project its vision of Islam around the world. Every year, billions of Saudi dollars are pumped into *madrasa*s (seminaries), mosques, and Islamic institutions worldwide that preach this particular creed. It is those billions, not bin Laden's allegedly great fortune, that have financed al-Qaeda and its small army of supporters in Afghanistan, Pakistan, and elsewhere. Thus, in formulating U.S. efforts to promote democracy in the Arab world, one must first come to terms with Saudi complicity in the bin Laden phenomenon—a complicity that operates at the highest levels of Saudi society and in a myriad of as-yet-unexamined ways.

These problems were illuminated in a recent article by Seymour Hersh entitled "King's Ransom" in the October 22, 2001, issue of the *New Yorker*. After studying electronic intercepts of communications between members of the Saudi royal family (obtained by the National Security Agency and leaked to him by the Central Intelligence Agency [CIA]), Hersh concluded that the regime is so corrupt, "so alienated from the country's religious rank and file, and so weakened and frightened that it has brokered its future by channeling hundreds of millions of dollars in what amounts to protection money to fundamentalist groups that wish to overthrow it." More specifically, Hersh argued, "The intercepts have demonstrated to analysts that by 1996 Saudi money was supporting Osama bin Laden's al-Qaeda and other extremist groups in Afghanistan, Lebanon, Yemen, and Central Asia, and throughout the Persian Gulf region." Hersh quoted an American intelligence official to support this claim: "'[1996] is the key year. . . . Bin Laden hooked up to all the bad guys—it's like the Grand Alliance—and had a capability for conducting large-scale operations. . . . [The Saudi regime had] gone to the dark side.'"

Hersh's article is the thin end of a wedge that I—speaking as an Arab, as a democrat, and as a Muslim—hope other journalists will pick up on and hammer home. Both American and Arab journalists should go for the jugular on this issue, and the best way to do so is to follow the money trail. Inevitably, some will raise legitimate doubts: "What if such investigations bring down the House of Saud? There are no democratic alternatives in Saudi Arabia. Who will take the place of the existing regime? Can America afford to undermine what has been the pillar of its foreign policy in the Middle East for so many decades?" To such questions I would answer, "After September 11, can America afford not to?"

The impasse of Saudi-U.S. relations in the wake of September 11 brings me to the case of Iraq, for whom 1996 was also a seminal year. This was the year in which the United States allowed Saddam Husayn to invade the city of Irbil in the supposedly protected area of northern Iraq. This was the year in which the United States acquiesced when the U.S.-based Iraqi opposition to Saddam was routed out of northern Iraq. This was the year in which 150 Iraqi democrats died in and around Irbil waiting for American air support that never came. Thus, 1996 is not only the year in which the Saudi regime went over to the "dark side"; it is also the year in which the CIA subverted a democratic agenda in Iraq in favor of a Saudi agenda of bringing about regime change through an officer-led coup, which would have replaced one set of Ba'athist faces in Iraq with another. The CIA kept this agenda from the opposition Iraqi National Congress (INC); the INC already knew of the planned coup, however, and warned the CIA that the conspiracy had been completely infiltrated by Saddam's agents. The CIA did not listen, however, and between 100 and 200 Iraqi officers were executed by Saddam in the summer of 1996. Henceforth, the INC—the only hope for fundamental regime change in Iraq—was the object of slander and ridicule in the United States, a campaign led first by the CIA and then by the State Department. The accusations and incitements against the Iraqi National Congress continue to this day, and their reverberations can be felt in the Bush administration and in the Departments of Defense and State as they debate U.S. policy toward Iraq.

Currently, evidence is mounting that Iraq may have played a role in the September 11 attacks. In an important sign of things to come, President George W. Bush recently named Abdul Rahman Yasin as one of the twenty-two most-wanted terrorists worldwide. Yasin is the shadowy figure who escaped to Baghdad after his alleged involvement in the first World Trade Center bombing in 1993. With the exception of Laurie Mylroie's recently updated book *The War against America: Saddam Hussein and the World Trade Center Attacks* (2001), little was said about Yasin before September 11. The photo of him released with the most-wanted list was supplied to Washington by the INC, which belies the INC's public portrayal as a London-based, "armchair" opposition group.

What is the specific Iraqi connection to bin Laden? Certainly, the seeds of September 11 were sown during the Gulf War. Obviously, though, evidence of a connection at the practical, operational level remains undefinitive. Should this lack of solid proof really matter? Iraq is, after all, a terrorist state, and the fact that it was permitted to stand in defiance of all that occurred during the Gulf War has contributed enormously to the climate of opinion in which the bin Ladens of this world thrive. Over the past ten years, Saddam Husayn has turned the U.S. military victory into a political defeat. It should come as no surprise, then, that bin Laden has placed what he calls "the suffering of Iraqi children"—the rhetoric of the Iraqi regime—second on his list of grievances against the United States. The top item on that list, of course, is his Wahhabi objection to the "pollutive" U.S. military presence in the Arabian peninsula, which was established largely in order to contain Saddam.

Iraq is the best example of why the United States should carefully excise the cancerous growth of extremism from the region. Iraq's infrastructure, its middle class, its education system, even its military-industrial complex—built as they were by a totalitarian regime—are reasons for thinking that a new kind of order can be set up there, just as was accomplished in Germany and Japan after World War II. This new order should ideally be nonmilitarist, secular, non–Arab nationalist, and federal in structure. Moreover, Iraq is the world's second-largest oil producer after Saudi Arabia, with vast untapped reserves; in other words, Iraq, unlike Afghanistan, can pay for its own reconstruction. Americans and Arabs desperately need a success story in the Middle East other than Israel. And Israelis themselves need it; whether they like it or not, they are condemned to live in that region, and after thirty years of occupation, they have come to resemble their neighbors in more ways than they would like to admit.

September 11 represents a huge challenge for the Arab and Muslim worlds, as formidable as anything they have had to face since the fall of the Ottoman Empire. At the moment, the Arab world is still in denial about what happened on that day. As a friend and former Muslim activist put it to me soon after the attacks, "It couldn't have been the Arabs—we aren't capable of it." Many Arabs think that Israel's Mossad, or even the United States itself, planned the attacks solely for the purpose of discrediting the Arab world. One widely believed rumor holds that the Mossad warned some 4,000 Jewish employees in the World Trade Center to vacate the buildings a few minutes before the first plane struck. Arabs are telling themselves such stories in order to distance themselves from all sense of urgency and responsibility. But such a mindset reflects a sense of hopelessness and despair, not contempt. The contempt that Martin Kramer described evolves at a later stage, among the operatives of bin Laden, for example. Re-

gardless of the cause, it is despair that drives people into organizations like al-Qaeda, which then brainwash them and fill them with
contempt. Despair is the swamp in which such organizations and
attitudes flourish.

Along with the Palestinians, Iraq stands at the brink of a chasm
today. It can breed democrats or a corps of new bin Ladens. A new
paradigm will have to be created, one that Arabs can cling to in order
to pull themselves away from the abyss that, by and large, they have
dug for themselves. Before September 11, outsiders could say, "To
hell with it—that's their responsibility." After September 11, no one
should be saying this.

11

Roger Harrison

I HAD THE HONOR OF SERVING as ambassador to Jordan, where an experiment in democracy had begun about eighteen months before my arrival; King Hussein bin Talal had reconstituted his long-moribund parliament and called for national elections in 1988. I will never forget the moment during my Senate confirmation hearing when I had to discuss this experiment. At one point, Senator Daniel Moynihan looked down his long, aristocratic nose at me—where I was shivering in my chair—and asked me my opinion of Jordanian democracy. I could tell by his manner that he did not have a very high opinion of it himself. Actually, I shared some of Senator Moynihan's cynicism about democracy in Jordan. Then, as now, the parliament consisted of a bicameral, appointive upper house and an elected lower house, but the electoral districts had been severely gerrymandered in order to underrepresent Palestinian Jordanians. This fact dampened voter turnout in the country's first election, particularly among the underrepresented groups.

Moreover, Jordan's constitution places the parliament under the authority of the king. In its first few weeks of existence, the parliament often resounded with speeches about the perfidy of the United States and the glories of Saddam Husayn, and, on several occasions, the king raised the prospect—in private, and perhaps solely for my benefit—of abolishing it again. He never did so, however, which was yet another sign of his wisdom. Although I had considered the parliament inconsequential, it showed itself in times of crisis to be quite important, if only because it served as a sounding board for opinions that I knew were rife in Jordanian society. By creating an outlet for public opinion, the parliament validated these opinions, thereby diffusing much of the pressure that might otherwise have been brought to bear on the Hashemite regime.

In those days, the U.S. embassy was located in downtown Amman on a major street, so it served as a convenient place for protestors to gather. Since protests were frequent, the police set up cordons down the street to keep demonstrators from coming through. There never seemed to be enough policemen to hold back a determined crowd, yet when these policemen said, "Stop," the protestors always obeyed. Examples like this suggested that a certain legitimacy accompanied the sketchy democratic system that the king had installed—a legitimacy that probably helped to keep such demonstrations from boiling over.

The king also had the foresight to make parliamentary representation constituency based rather than proportional, allowing groups such as the Muslim Brotherhood to run for seats and obtain a voice in the parliament. This had an interesting effect, one that I witnessed firsthand. Because these new representatives had constituencies, they were forced to respond to the demands of political life. In fact, their constituents often besieged them in the parliament building itself. The power of direct democracy has always impressed me; I had seen it in London years before, when I followed a parliamentarian during his election campaign and watched constituents grab him and complain about all of their problems, whether it was in his power to fix them or not.

Eventually, this process served to demythologize the Muslim Brotherhood in Jordan. Outside of parliament, they were representatives of pure Islam. Inside parliament, however, they had to do those "impure" things that politicians do in order to serve their constituencies—which brought them down to a more human level and helped to put their movement in perspective. Occasionally, the Brotherhood has refused to participate in the political process. They are ambivalent about it themselves, in part because of this demythologizing effect.

Long before my firsthand experiences with democratization in the Middle East, I had regarded it as a mission, of sorts. I first came to Washington at a time when "idealist" was something you were, not something you called people you disliked. Idealists were the norm in the 1960s; we came to Washington with the conviction that spreading democracy was something the United States should do, and with the equally strong conviction that we had the ability to do it. We had that good-old American know-how, and a moral impulse to do what we said we could do.

In many ways, though, U.S. foreign policy since that time has been informed by a tension between the moral impulse toward democratization and the kind of cynicism that makes efforts along that line seem doomed to failure. This tension was evident, for example, in the Clinton administration's agony over Bosnia. Similarly, it has long clouded America's efforts to determine the direction in which its moral compass should point in the Middle East. More important, this tension is visible today, as people argue that the U.S. campaign against terrorism must involve more than just a war—that some form of constructive engagement must be included in any policy that seeks to create a terrorism-free world. So the issue of democratization is very much alive, and the problem now becomes one of balancing this liberalizing tendency with the demands that realism imposes on us, all toward developing the most effective foreign policy possible.

To what extent can we fulfill this American dream of doing good in the world by spreading democratic values? Over the years, I have come to believe that changing the social systems and ideologies of other countries is probably beyond the capabilities of the United States; its past attempts to do so have led to violence more often than would be coincidence. Thus, any present or future administration should be very careful about trying to reorder the political landscape. At the same time, it is not inevitably true that Americans cannot or should not take decisive and forcible action against those who are hostile toward democracy; sometimes such action is necessary to further their national aspirations. Ho Chi Minh may have died in his bed, ripe with years and full of honors, but Slobodan Milosevic is in jail, where he belongs.

In many respects, democratization has been taken out of America's hands. There are forces working in the world and against various regimes (e.g., the House of Saud) that are neither strictly local nor beholden to any specific U.S. policy, but are instead the result of the free movement of people and ideas that we call globalization. This phenomenon has put extraordinary pressure on authoritarian, hierarchical governments all over the world. Such governments are finding that they are unable to satisfy the basic demands of their citizenry without taking some of the steps that the United States has been nagging them about for years: enfranchising their citizens, paying attention to public opinion, opening their markets and banking systems, ending corruption, and so forth. Globalization has required these governments to address, however belatedly, many of the elements in the U.S. message of democratization and liberalization.

Thus, America now finds itself at one of those rare points in history in which it can do well by doing good. That is, it can promote democracy and positive social change around the world simply by continuing the movement toward globalization that it has been so energetic in facilitating over the last ten years. Of course, this may not be an easy process, or one that proceeds without further violence. To paraphrase Hegel: "History isn't made without pain. Happy times are blank pages in history." The United States will experience some pain as this historical process unfolds. Yet, if Americans resist the nativist tendency to turn back in on themselves—to dismantle the systems of globalization that are in their own and the world's best interests—they will bring about the ideals that inspired them all those years ago. In other words, America should not quit while it is ahead.

12

Amy W. Hawthorne

I COME TO THESE ISSUES not as an outsider or an academic, but as someone who has worked with them on a practical basis for several years in an effort to promote democracy in the Arab world. As the title of this panel suggests, we are primarily concerned with "principles and interests"; the central question then becomes, "Do they intersect, and if so, how?" For many years, U.S. principles (e.g., freedom, democracy, tolerance, pluralism) and U.S. interests in the Arab world (e.g., stability, continuance of the status quo) rarely intersected in discussions about U.S. Middle East policy. Instead, U.S. policy toward this region has most often been marked by cold, hard realpolitik, which in many cases seemed to have been the best short-term course of action.

In the aftermath of September 11, however, more people are starting to ask whether promoting U.S. principles in the region promotes U.S. interests as well. Is the shortage of democracy in the Middle East directly, or even indirectly, responsible for what happened on September 11? Can the United States avoid similar attacks by trying to change the negative conditions in the Arab world? Such questions have prompted rhetoric throughout Washington about remaking the region, spreading U.S. values, teaching people not to hate America, and even developing a "Marshall Plan" for the Middle East. I would like to bring the rhetoric down from the clouds to a more practical level.

When Americans talk about democracy promotion in any part of the world, they tend to regard it in one of two ways: either as an inherently good impulse that does not need to be thought through, or as a horribly misguided impulse that should not be acted upon. The truth, however, lies somewhere in between. Finding this truth requires one to answer several important questions: Would more democracy in the Arab world help decrease the appeal of terrorism for those in the region? If so, what is the role of the United States in promoting democracy? How has the United States tried to promote

81

it in the past? What lessons can be drawn from these past efforts in order to improve future efforts, particularly if policymakers decide to make democracy promotion a higher priority?

Democracy is, in fact, a big part of the answer to the problems in the Middle East. Nothing would be more favorable to long-term U.S. interests than an Arab world full of smoothly functioning, stable democracies with free market economies and good educational systems. The challenge lies not in determining whether democracy itself serves U.S. interests, but in accepting the process of democratization that is needed to reach this result. Americans often forget how their own democracy developed—how difficult it is for democracy to take root, and how it often involves political upheaval, instability, and violently competing forces. Pondering what kinds of changes might take place in the Middle East if real democratization occurs can be quite unnerving, but it is essential.

Americans must also develop a better understanding of the actual state of political reform in the region. The political landscape of the Arab world is much maligned. As Freedom House points out, the region is home to more undemocratic regimes than any other part of the world. Yet, the Arab world is not completely barren of political reform. It is not like North Korea, which is a stagnant, closed entity. Many parts of the region have changed dramatically over the past thirty years. For example, things are being said and done in Egypt today that would have been unthinkable in the Nasser era, or even under Anwar Sadat. Initial steps toward liberalization were taken throughout the region more than a decade ago: the first multiparty elections, parliaments, and nongovernmental organizations (NGOs); increased public discussion of issues such as corruption and human rights; the rise of new media outlets such as al-Jazeera; and regional debate about whether democracy is good for the Middle East.

This process, however, is incomplete. The region is full of raised expectations, but also frustration, cynicism, and dashed hopes. The promise of change has not fully developed there. The form of democracy is in place, but not the substance. One sees first competitive elections, but not second. NGO leaders are permitted to speak out, but then are put in prison. Americans must understand these real conditions whenever they talk about promoting democracy in the

Middle East. The lack of optimism in the region—the lack of belief that democracy can really take hold there—is striking. And democracy is, in the end, a matter of optimism. Americans play the democratic game day after day because they believe in the future; if they lose one day, they know that they can compete again some other day. This faith is lacking in the Arab world. If the United States decides to promote democracy there, it must recognize that the transition—the democratization process—will pose challenges to its interests. There will be bumps along the road—regimes that America supports now may not last, new forces may emerge, and so forth.

From a practical standpoint, effective democracy promotion consists of several different elements, regardless of the region in question. One of these elements is the power of example. That is, the United States can do a great deal to foster democracy simply by being itself: by serving as a leading example of democratic values and freedom around the world. This holds true even in the Arab world; despite well-publicized anti-Americanism, many in the region still admire the United States. At the same time, though, Middle Easterners and others view Americans through their own local lenses, and inevitably, the U.S. example of democracy is often diluted by some antipathy toward U.S. foreign policy. Although at present there is no real solution for this dilemma, it must be acknowledged.

A second element of democracy promotion is diplomacy, which requires the U.S. government to use its bilateral relationships as a platform for raising issues related to democratization. Using both carrots and sticks, the United States can encourage other countries to undertake reforms. The U.S. relationship with Russia during the 1990s shows the potential successes and pitfalls of this kind of diplomatic approach to democracy promotion.

A third element is actual democracy aid. This is the nitty-gritty level of democracy promotion: providing practical assistance. This element often has a certain romantic appeal; most Americans are attracted to the idea of spreading democracy, encouraging free elections, sharing their values, helping democrats in other countries speak out. Unfortunately, past efforts have not been very effective; when it comes to actual implementation, these ideas usually do not work out as intended. In sum, if the United States is going to undertake effective, large-scale democracy promotion in the Arab world, it must employ all of the above elements simultaneously.

In the end, however, democratic reform is an internal process. The United States cannot simply transplant its civil society to other countries, no matter how good its intentions or how strong its will. Democratization efforts in the Middle East will succeed or fail based on the aspirations and actions of the people who live there. This fact is often forgotten in democracy promotion. Many in the field believe that if they just try hard enough, they can convince other countries to adopt democratic characteristics. Real democratic reform does not work that way, though. The United States is an external actor—albeit a powerful one—and its attempts to influence the political cultures of other countries are often felt only at the margins. For example, some of the fledgling political openings of the 1990s—such as the Jordanian, Qatari, or Yemeni experiments with liberalization—occurred on their own, independent of direct American demands or the efforts of the international community. The United States would do well to look for these kinds of independent developments and support them, without the illusion that it can force democratic reform.

Americans must also remember that democratic reform is not a neutral process. For one thing, it involves extremely sensitive internal political issues and intersects with questions of national sovereignty; locals often see democracy promotion as a form of meddling. Moreover, when the United States intervenes in favor of a particular political process or outcome, it is inevitably lending support to one group or another, intentionally or not. Americans regard their efforts along these lines as inherently good, but the locals rarely feel the same way; after all, if democratization is truly at work, someone is going to lose, and someone will win. The process is defined by changing political power.

The United States can also learn from its past efforts to encourage political reform in the region. Global democracy promotion was a major foreign policy theme of the Clinton administration during the 1990s, at least rhetorically. It was one of the major international goals toward which Bill Clinton promised to work upon assuming office. And his agenda did, in fact, trickle down to the Middle East. The U.S. government was more engaged on issues of local reform, both with friends of the United States and with countries that were not so friendly. The administration spoke more often and somewhat more publicly of civil society, pluralism, and elections. Its human rights reports became more accurate as policymakers increasingly began to address this issue.

These efforts extended to actual democracy aid, as the United States spent more than $350 million during the 1990s on a variety of democratization programs throughout the region, including Egypt, the West Bank, Gaza, Morocco, Algeria, Tunisia, Lebanon, and Yemen. Although this was less than half of what was spent on similar programs in sub-Saharan Africa, it was still a fairly significant amount—in light of the fact that almost nothing had been spent on democracy promotion in the region during previous decades. These funds were used for a variety of projects: training Palestinian Legislative Council members, observing elections in Algeria, fostering civic dialogue in Morocco, computerizing court systems in Egypt, teaching U.S. campaign methods to Yemeni political parties, and so forth.

Generally speaking, the United States applied the same template of democracy promotion to the Arab world that it had used in Eastern Europe, Russia, sub-Saharan Africa, and Latin America. That is, it often focused on strengthening institutions that resembled its own: congresses, parliaments, political parties, judicial systems, and NGOs. The rationale behind this approach was that by improving the technical effectiveness of potentially democratic institutions in Arab countries, the United States could somehow prepare these countries for the onset of democracy itself. According to this theory, procedurally sound parliaments and well-run NGOs were crucial factors in encouraging democratization. This approach did, in fact, have positive effects; some good training programs were developed, some new ideas were introduced, and some brave democrats in the region were supported through these initiatives. Yet, the approach did not encourage any deep structural change. In some cases, even the best initiatives were washed away by much stronger forces. For example, some of the programs established with the Palestinian Legislative Council in the West Bank and Gaza ran fairly well. Yet, the relevance of these programs was lost in the broader turmoil of Palestinian politics.

Why did these efforts have relatively little impact in the Arab world? The region itself has long presented several daunting obstacles to democracy promotion, many of which have gained increased attention since September 11. For one thing, due to widespread anti-American sentiment, there are few credible local partners who will readily engage with the United States in such efforts. Moreover, the U.S. government maintains close relationships with several undemocratic leaders in the region; U.S. officials believe that it is no small challenge to encourage political reform among such allies without disrupting the many other important elements of those relationships.

Another shortcoming in the U.S. approach was the fact that people in the region did not see the democracy promotion initiatives as connected to a larger policy. Many local activists believed that if they went out on a limb and did what U.S. programs were encouraging them to do—that is, if they spoke out in the press, or established their own NGOs, or otherwise followed through on U.S. democratization training—the U.S. government would not support them in the end. And indeed, if such activity created awkwardness or tension at the diplomatic level, Washington would, more often than not, dampen its support. It should come as no surprise, then, that some in the region fail to take U.S. pledges of support for democracy seriously.

In addition, many of these programs were based on U.S. ideas, initiatives, and assessments, not on the stated needs of Middle Easterners themselves. This tendency can be attributed to several factors—the bureaucratic imperatives of U.S. foreign assistance, lack of creativity within the democracy promotion community, and so forth—but the end result was that the locals involved in the U.S.-initiated programs did not always feel that they had ownership, and they therefore grew cynical about the whole endeavor. For example, U.S. aid workers would arrive in a country and ask, with typical American naivete and the best of intentions, "Would you like us to provide training for your political parties?" At first, the locals would answer, "Yes, absolutely." In private, however, they would say to each other, "Well, maybe we'll get a trip to the United States out of this, or some computer equipment. We'll go along with it." In other words, they were not fully committed to what the United States was actually trying to achieve through these programs, largely because many of the initiatives were not well designed.

Even when the locals were genuinely interested in U.S. democratization programs, they often found it difficult to apply them in their own political contexts. Some of these programs were based on a misunderstanding of political power and the possible avenues of reform in the Arab world, and were not fully adapted to local conditions. For example, one multiyear U.S. program aimed, among other objectives, to encourage the Egyptian parliament to initiate legislation more often, as a counterweight to the executive branch. In the abstract, this seemed to be a sound proposal, modeled on the strong role played by the U.S. Congress. The Egyptian parliament, however, is unlikely to develop this attribute; the structure of the Egyptian political system does not favor such a change, as the preponderance of power rests with the executive branch, not the parliament.

In other cases, the U.S. government saw democracy assistance as a means of supporting particular individuals in particular countries—political leaders with whom it wanted to develop closer ties, or individuals who appeared to be reformers, but who were not necessarily perceived as such locally. Thus, many in the Arab world saw these democratization programs as America's way of bolstering decidedly undemocratic individuals; the United States was providing moral and material support to those who were not viewed as genuine agents of change in their own countries.

In the future, the United States must take its democracy promotion efforts in the Arab world much more seriously. Such programs must be designed more effectively and integrated within larger policy concerns. They should be part of a vision, one that is articulated in public and in private and followed through with on the ground. The U.S. government must prepare itself for some uncomfortable discussions with its regional partners about what sorts of reforms it considers necessary, and about how it will assist in implementing these reforms.

At the same time, the United States must realize that it cannot be the engine of democratic reform in the Middle East. At best, Americans can help to set the agenda for such reform and nurture those local forces that will carry it out. Washington can encourage change, but it will not be the ultimate catalyst, despite its power and influence; that step is the responsibility of those in the region. Americans have a short memory about how their own democracy developed.

Even if Arabs embark on large-scale democracy promotion with U.S. support, it will take at least a generation for such measures to achieve fruition and fundamental change. The challenge of external democracy promotion—as well as its critical importance—must be acknowledged from the outset.

13

Discussion

Robert B. Satloff, *The Washington Institute:* Let us assume that U.S. democracy promotion efforts should be focused on nations. That is, the United States does not want to foster a single "Arabism" that erases national boundaries, or provide democracy to "the Arab world" in general; America's goal is to improve conditions in individual states. Therefore, some prioritization is necessary, and the task becomes one of determining which states to focus on first. If you had to advise President Bush on which Middle Eastern countries would benefit most from democratization efforts, where would you begin? Would you tell him to start with the fully authoritarian states (e.g., Iraq), reasoning that since they are the most egregious rights violators, American democratization programs would have the most immediate and positive effect? Or would you tell him to start with the relatively liberal states (e.g., Jordan), since change of a more evolutionary nature is possible there? Which, if either, of these approaches do you think is the right one for the United States?

Amy W. Hawthorne: The problem with either approach is that it may not be a good idea to concentrate on a single state—friendly or hostile—while ignoring others in the region. In other parts of the world, the United States has had some success in promoting democracy by applying its efforts to many different countries simultaneously. Different levels and types of support can be offered at different times, but it would not be wise to focus on just one country.

The region desperately needs a success story, so the United States should focus most of its efforts on places where an impact might actually be made, or where the people are receptive to U.S. support. The Middle East has exhibited some internal momentum for this kind of change.

Michael Stein, *The Washington Institute:* Approaching democratization on a regional basis may not be the best route; that is a vast and complicated proposition, not likely to be handled successfully. Suppose that I were President Bush, and democracy promotion experts approached me saying, "The Middle East is the most undemocratic region on earth, and this fact will pose major problems for us both now and in the future. We have to plant democracy there one way or another." In reply, I would probably tell them to show me one place where they could do it: create one demonstration project, one successful democratization program. I would tell them to avoid tinkering with any of the countries with whom we have good relations, even if they are not true democracies. For instance, Jordan is not a perfect democracy, but given our solid relationship with the regime, we should be content to leave them alone for now. Egypt is too complicated a case to handle at the moment. The religious fanaticism in Saudi Arabia makes democratization efforts too risky there.

But what about Iraq? Now there is a nation that is ripe for a full-scale democratization campaign. The U.S. government wants to depose Saddam Husayn anyway, and the potential downsides and risks are minimal; it is difficult to conceive that the result of any regime change could be worse than the current situation. The United States should focus all of its efforts on Iraq: a massive campaign, properly funded and involving all of its resources, both domestic and Iraqi. Such an effort has the best chance of succeeding, and may even produce a ripple effect throughout the Middle East. Otherwise, the United States will be left with the tinkering, scattershot approach that has yet to produce significant gains. America should focus on one country, put all of its power to work there, make sure that it succeeds, and then wait to see what developments arise as a result of its success.

Hawthorne: Although having a different regime in Iraq would certainly be a good thing, history shows that the impulse to replace the old with the new often produces unexpected—and negative—results. If Saddam were deposed, there is no guarantee that democracy would automatically fill the void. We need to disabuse ourselves of the illusion that if we simply sweep away a problem, its replacement will necessarily constitute a sea change.

A similar line of thinking was sparked by the emergence of a new generation of reformist rulers in the Middle East, such as

Bashar al-Asad in Syria, King Mohammed VI in Morocco, and King Abdullah II in Jordan. Their ascension to power generated great hope and raised expectations of dramatic change throughout the region. People felt that these regime changes alone would be immediately transformative; that the countries in question would "modernize" themselves quickly, opening their societies and experimenting with different economic structures. True reform does not work that way, though. These young rulers may in fact have a profound effect, but not instantaneously.

Moreover, we cannot ignore a country like Egypt simply because its problems are so daunting and the prospects for immediate change so unlikely. Yes, it is the most politically difficult nation in which to pursue democratic reform, but doing so is critically important.

Hilal Khashan, *American University of Beirut:* Regarding Iraq, Kanan's earlier comparison of that country to Japan and Germany is problematic. First of all, when democracy was introduced in Japan and Germany, those two countries had, at one point or another, already achieved highly developed economies and a strong sense of nationalism and political community. Even so, their democratic governments have not really been tested over the past fifty years, so their future stability is not a certainty.

Far less credible is the notion of promoting American democracy in Iraq—an idea that has gained much attention in the years since the Gulf War. Democracy is not a commodity to be promoted. It requires certain behavioral characteristics that are alien to the Iraqi environment. Moreover, Iraq is not really a unified state in the democratic sense. Shi'is compose the majority in the south of the country, Arab Sunnis in the center, and Kurds in the north. How could a democratic order—that is, majority rule—ever be applied to Iraq? Do we really think, for example, that the Sunnis and Kurds would allow the Shi'is to preside over them?

Between the two world wars, the British promoted liberalism and democracy in Iraq, but the Iraqi political parties and the army made a mockery of it. To make things worse, the army staged a Nazi-oriented military coup in 1941. I therefore find it extremely difficult to believe that a population embittered by years of adventurism and emaciated by hunger will be able to think democratically in the near future. The first step is to instill the idea of nationhood there; the various groups must agree on a form of government and accept the idea of Iraq as a unified, permanent state.

Kanan Makiya: In the case of Iraq, fundamental, structural regime change would require several ideological reversals—first, a movement away from Arab nationalism and militarism. A truly new regime would also have to be openly plural, or at least federal—the latter alternative has actually been discussed at length and voted for by the Iraqi opposition and the Kurds. I was present at those discussions in 1992, so I know that federalism is a real option in Iraq; the Kurds certainly want it. Although federalism is not democracy, it is a step in an interesting direction. Any new regime would also have to rest on some system of law. Which system should be established is an open question, but rule of law is not too much to ask.

We must remember that in the case of Iraq, regime change is not simply one option among many. The country is in dire straits, facing a collapse of the very fabric of its society. Clearly, the regime of Saddam Husayn is not a permanent part of the landscape, regardless of whether or not the United States takes action against it. Regime change is almost certainly going to occur, but it can happen in a number of different ways. As others have pointed out, many of these means would likely make the situation worse. Such scenarios can be avoided only through deliberate, voluntary action on the part of individuals to construct a better government. Those who desire positive regime change have an obligation to develop and implement this construction, in whatever manner possible. And this does not mean copying those methods that were used in postwar Germany and Japan; that analogy is useful, but analogies are sometimes dangerous.

Hilal made another important point in questioning whether Iraqis have any sense of national identity. This factor would play a major role in the success or failure of any attempts at regime change. I think that such an identity does in fact exist, and that it was partially forged by the Iraq-Iran war. For example, the Shi'is of Iraq may not have wanted to fight that war, but they did. By and large, they did not defect as Iran had hoped they would, even after eight years of warfare and massive suffering. The experience of living under Saddam's regime may well have strengthened their sense of Iraqi identity. Still, this factor remains an unknown.

In the wake of September 11, the rules of engagement in the Middle East have been completely altered. America has to think big, and to consider dramatic action, if it is to prevent the region from sinking further. Many of the most fundamental elements of the regional order are changing. For one thing, it appears as if the Saudi pillar of American Middle East policy is about to undergo a shakeup, perhaps within the next few years. If this does happen, it will constitute an enormous change in the region as a whole. The United States must prepare for such change—for the prospect that the rampant corruption within the House of Saud may have helped to create the monster that perpetrated the September 11 attacks.

The recent diplomatic snafu between New York City mayor Rudolph Giuliani and Saudi prince Al Waleed Bin Talal—in which the mayor rejected the prince's $10-million relief donation after the latter implicitly linked the attacks to America's role in the Israeli-Palestinian conflict—is but a microcosm of the kind of changes that might occur in U.S.-Saudi relations in the near future. Such changes would be akin to pulling the rug out from under American Middle East policy. This policy was in shambles even before September 11, however, so it is high time for the United States to adopt a fresh approach. Again, the first step should be fundamental change in Iraq—not necessarily by bombing the country, but by working with Iraqis.

Roger Harrison: It is interesting to read the biographies of those who had to decide how far into Iraq U.S. forces would go in February 1991; by choosing to hold back, they sparked a debate that is still being waged today. They defended their decision by appealing to the need to preserve international consensus, but I have always suspected that the real impediment for them was that they had no idea what they would have done had they marched into Baghdad. They had no Douglas MacArthur to sort things out for them. The current administration does not seem to have any firmer sense of how to solve the problem, and this uncertainty serves as a strong argument against becoming embroiled in a situation that it will be unable to sort out.

Fred Schwartz, *The Washington Institute:* Several years ago, I attended an economic conference in Jordan. During one discussion, an Israeli stood up and said, "I've noticed that a lot of sixteen-wheeler trucks come up from Aqaba, then move through Amman and on to Iraq; things would be a lot more efficient with the building of a high-speed railroad." A Jordanian in the audience stood up and replied, "Over my dead body"; it turns out that he owned the trucks. This illustrates what was said earlier about the difficulties of U.S. development efforts (including democracy promotion); too often, the United States fails to account for those crucial local details that impede its initiatives, and its efforts are therefore seen as meddling.

Most Americans believe in asserting democracy because they see it as the most efficient way for nations to govern themselves and for humanity to thrive. Nevertheless, the U.S. approach to democratization is inherently limited because Americans often lack intimate knowledge of the countries that they are trying to reform—of the local customs, modes of behavior, and so forth.

Is there a way to refocus this strategy? To concentrate on those characteristics of democratic nations that have universal appeal and can transcend national and cultural differences? For example, the United States could focus on offering material aid and guidance in areas like health care or education. Eventually, such efforts may foster beneficial social principles and behaviors, and the countries in question would then be ripe for the introduction of democratic ideas.

Bernard Lewis, *Princeton University:* The Western world suffers from the rather pathetic illusion that democracy is the natural and normal condition of mankind, and that any deviation from this condition is either a disease to be cured or a crime to be punished. But this is not so. What Westerners call "democracy" simply consists of the parochial habits that English-speaking peoples have adopted for the conduct of their public affairs. These habits have spread to a few other countries, but only a few. If one were to make a list of countries in which democracy has functioned smoothly for the last century—and where it will likely continue to function smoothly for the next—one would have a very short list indeed. Such a list would exclude, for example, most of continental Europe, except perhaps

Scandinavia, the Netherlands, and Switzerland. The West must rid itself of this idea and accept the fact that democracy is simply one way of doing things. It is not the only way, and in many parts of the world, it is not necessarily the best way.

Similarly, Westerners have a tendency to assume that there are two kinds of government in the world—democratic and undemocratic—and to lump all of the undemocratic governments together in one undifferentiated mass of tyranny when there are, in fact, enormous differences between them. Some undemocratic governments are civilized, humane, and conducted under law, and their citizens have rights that are respected by this law. They may not choose or change their leaders in the same manner as does the United States, but this does not mean that they are tyrannies.

The notion of exporting democratic institutions is not new. During the days of colonial rule in the Middle East, the British and the French tried very hard to plant their own types of democracy in the region; the British established constitutional monarchies, the French unstable republics. None of them worked—they have collapsed and fallen all over the Middle East. The only place in the Islamic Middle East where democracy seems to be working is in Turkey, which of course is the one Muslim country in the region that was never subject to foreign domination. Granted, the Turks are having a hard time of it; their democracy has been punctuated by many reverses and upheavals. Nevertheless, it is functioning and developing.

In his 1991 book *The Third Wave: Democratization in the Late Twentieth Century*, Samuel Huntington wrote that a country can be called a democracy only when it has changed its government twice by election. Sometimes, either on principle or through inadvertence, a government allows itself to be voted out of power. Their replacements, however, will do everything they can to ensure that they do not go out in the same manner; thus, Huntington's "twice" is important. In Turkey, the government has been changed many times by election. It has been changed by other methods as well, but the elections are what count.

Colonial India is another remarkable case. There, the democratic institutions established by the imperial power were inherited by the successor states. In modern India, these institutions have continued to function after more than half a century and many troubles. In Pakistan, however, they have a very checkered history. Does this mean that democracy cannot work in an Islamic country? Not at all. But Muslims must develop democracy in ways that are in conformity with their traditions. Many elements in the Islamic tradition are, in fact, conducive to the development of democratic institutions. For example, the principle of sovereignty, according to Islamic doctrine, is both consensual and contractual. The principle that there is a law above the government—whether one calls it "divine law" or "the constitution"—is essentially the same in Muslim and Western thought, and this belief was respected in the classical Islamic state. In many modern Islamic nations, however, we find a special kind of tyranny that results from failed democracies, as was seen earlier in continental Europe.

Harrison: I agree that some nondemocratic systems have functioned very well. Yet, the rules of the game seem to be changing, and some regimes that have functioned well in the past may not function so well now. For example, consider the trends in Saudi Arabian public opinion over the last decade. Ten years ago, it would have been very difficult to find a Saudi who had heard of the *New Yorker*. Today, however, I imagine that many Saudis have read, for example, Seymour Hersh's recent *New Yorker* article on their royal family, which Kanan described earlier. This illustrates a fundamental change in certain Middle Eastern societies, one that may reveal their regimes to be less stable and resilient than the West thinks they are.

Simon Henderson, *Saudi Strategies:* I was surprised that, unlike Professor Lewis, none of the panelists mentioned rule of law in their presentations. Moreover, none of them mentioned the most vibrant example of an imperfect democracy in the Middle East—Iran—probably because it is so irritating.

More to the point, the fundamental barrier to U.S. democracy promotion efforts in the Middle East is that the United States has an image problem in the region. First, the citizens of many Middle Eastern countries are permitted to criticize the United States publicly, routinely, and vehemently, in part so that they do not criticize their own regimes. Second, many of the media through which this criticism is channeled (e.g., political cartoons) tend to depict America as a man driving a tank or piloting a warplane. The United States should be trying to transform that depiction to one of Lady Justice, with her scales in one hand and her sword of justice in the other. This change is not occurring at present, though, and given today's panel presentations, I cannot see it happening anytime in the near future.

Azar Nafisi, *Johns Hopkins University, School of Advanced International Studies Dialogue Project:* Iran is indeed an interesting example. Certainly, that country has offered the clearest formulation of modern theocracy and modern fundamentalist rule. But Iran has made no significant progress in becoming truly democratic; more important, it has even failed to become a truly theocratic state. This failure raises many questions about Islam and reformation, questions that would have been *verboten* twenty years ago. Witness the many Islamic clerics, even in Iran, who are currently questioning old assumptions about Islamic rule. It may be useful, then, to view Iran as a sort of Soviet Union in the Middle East, in the sense that the regime is questioning its own ideological foundations.

As for democracy promotion in general, the United States must carefully consider the manner in which it presents its democratic alternatives to the region. For example, Americans should look more closely at the notion of their businesses taking democracy in tow with them when they set up shop in countries like Iran. Does AOL really take democracy to China or Iran when it operates there? What about Exxon or Mobil, or any other corporation?

Pamela Reeves, *independent democracy consultant:* From a practical standpoint, how ready or willing is the United States to implement Islam-specific democracy promotion in the wake of September 11? The democratization community prides itself on being value-neutral. Yet, has the United States or any of its allies ever done rule-of-law programming when the law in question is *shari'a*? Inevitably, Western democratization planners are going to run up against cultural elements that they have never seen before and have no idea how to handle.

Moreover, the United States must be careful not to forget the non-Arab world. Non–Middle Eastern countries that are receiving American democracy aid now may lose it as the United States begins to focus more of its attention on the Arab world. Particularly worrisome are countries that border Arab states (e.g., Chad) and those that are on the brink of collapse for socioeconomic, political, or geographic reasons. The United States currently spends something like $700 million per year on democracy assistance, and it must determine whether these funds can be equitably distributed on a global basis in the post–September 11 world.

Daniel Sagalyn, NewsHour with Jim Lehrer: If elections were held in Saudi Arabia six months from now, who would come to power? Would the new regime be friendly toward the United States? What kinds of domestic policies and core beliefs would characterize its rule?

Hawthorne: To a certain extent, the result would depend on the nature of the elections. Even if they were run properly, it would be nearly impossible to predict their outcome. Perhaps the Saudi people would want more of the same governance. They might be more comfortable with what they already have than with the unknown.

Makiya: Those who support or think like Osama bin Laden would probably win any such election.

PART FIVE

Middle East Terrorists with 'Global Reach': From Hizballah to Egyptian Islamic Jihad

14

Mamoun Fandy

WELL BEFORE SEPTEMBER 11, the world was experiencing at least five major global flows: 1) increased movement of people to and from all parts of the world; 2) proliferation of media and information; 3) accelerated financial movement; 4) increased movement of technology; and 5) increased weapons transfers. Filtering the terrorist movements out of the general flow—separating legitimate activities from illegitimate activities, terrorist money from legal money—is at the heart of the fight against terrorism.

In 1979, when I was a junior at Asiut University in southern Egypt, a political science graduate there named Mohammad Sa'id Habib wrote a paper about jihad and America. In hindsight, it is clear to me that the Islamist war against the United States began with that document. At the time, however, I had no idea that it would become, more or less by 1996, the foundation for Osama bin Laden's declaration of jihad against America, and later against "the Jews and the Crusaders," as he put it.

The year 1979 was also significant in the Middle East for other reasons; with the outbreak of the Islamic Revolution in Iran, many societies in the region became stages for conflict between Leftist and Islamic ideas. Egyptian president Anwar Sadat decided that he would support the Islamists against the Leftists in Egypt, and with that decision came the emergence of Islamic Jihad and of other Muslim groups throughout Egyptian universities. These are the very same groups that produced Sadat's assassin in 1981. That same year, Ayman al-Zawahiri—who later became Osama bin Laden's number-two lieutenant—could be seen at Asiut University trying to recruit students for his cause. At the time, Egyptians were ambivalent about fundamentalism in general, and about the Islamization of society; even after Sadat's assassination, some Egyptians continued to flirt with these ideas. With Israel's 1982 invasion of Lebanon, Arab politics created an additional context for the rise to prominence of these movements in the hearts and minds of many people.

The major event that led to the emergence of Osama bin Laden, though, was Iraq's invasion of Kuwait in 1990. This event enhanced the culture of ambivalence in the Arab world, with many wavering in their sympathies for each side. Indeed, many condemned Saddam Husayn's invasion, but others saw him as liberating the Palestinian territories via Kuwait, just as bin Laden's more recent terrorist attacks have been portrayed as an attempt to liberate the Palestinians. Media outlets such as the al-Jazeera television network appear to vacillate between airing such views and providing more legitimate coverage.

The Egyptian view of terrorism was long characterized by the same ambivalence. From 1980 to 1995, most Egyptians were more or less undecided about terrorism. They compared the corruption of the existing government to those who, with the Qur'an in one hand, were trying to establish a just society in Egypt. During this period, a furious debate between secular government and Islamic forces was waged in Egyptian newspapers, radio, and television. Years passed before the regime was able to convince Egyptians that its effort against certain Islamic extremist groups was simply the struggle of a Muslim government against terrorism. This fact should be taken very seriously by the United States as it tries to make the case that it is fighting terrorism, not Islam. If it took President Hosni Mubarak several years to convince his own people, I am not sure how long it will take the United States to drive this point home to other Muslim societies.

A second lesson from Egypt is that those who supported the Islamic groups were linking many of the groups' actions with issues such as civil liberties and human rights. At the same time, many felt that the Egyptian government was not doing enough to punish the criminal activities of these groups. President Mubarak did not win significant support from those who felt this way until he took decisive action against groups such as Islamic Jihad during the early 1990s, actually crushing these organizations by the middle of the decade. Yet, this victory drove individuals such as Ayman al-Zawahiri of Islamic Jihad into Sudan, Afghanistan, Bosnia, and Chechnya, so that the Egyptian problem became everyone else's problem. The same ambivalent linkage of the jihad movement with issues such as human rights was thereby solidified as a global phenomenon.

In the mid-1990s, bin Laden and al-Zawahiri were part of the grand conference that Hassan al-Turabi of Sudan convened in Khartoum. This conference included Imad Mughniyeh, a chief player within Hizballah, and bin Laden himself was featured as the main speaker. So the alliance between al-Qaeda and Islamic Jihad actually began in Sudan, although it was not formalized until al-Zawahiri moved to Afghanistan. In 1996, the United States and Saudi Arabia pressured Sudan to expel bin Laden and the Islamic groups that, a year earlier, had tried to assassinate President Mubarak in Ethiopia. Yet, the brief Sudanese experience was important in solidifying the merger between the jihad movement and Osama bin Laden.

The roots of that merger also lay in the 1993 attack on the World Trade Center, which led to the arrest of Shaykh Omar Abdul Rahman. Later on, Rahman's son was one of the main figures present in Afghanistan for the multiparty signing of bin Laden's 1998 declaration against "the Jews and the Crusaders." The globalization and fusion of these movements was further expanded by the attacks on the U.S. embassies in Africa later that year.

Today, we are faced with two rough categories of terrorist groups: those with patrons, and those without. Groups like Hizballah and Hamas are accountable to states, and America and its allies can make those states pay the price of supporting terrorism. Yet, groups without patrons are much more dangerous, particularly al-Qaeda and the Islamic Jihad movement, which severed their relationships with once-supportive regimes.

So the lessons from Egypt have some immediate implications for the current campaign against terrorism. For instance, the Arab world is still ambivalent about terrorism; witness the many who have described Osama bin Laden as an illegitimate figure hijacking the legitimate cause of Palestinian militancy. If the United States decides to target movements like Hizballah and Hamas in Phase II of the campaign, it will have a difficult time making a case against these groups in the Arab world.

Terrorist groups with "global reach" have long thrived on specific global issues, and many of these issues remain unresolved. Such groups echo widely held political grievances, and unless the world is firm in denying the use of terrorism as a means of expressing these ideas, many will become ambivalent about the fight against terror. Bin Laden may not be the appropriate mouthpiece to voice these grievances, but they are real and need to be addressed in order to deny terrorist groups justification for their actions and recruits for their causes.

Moreover, any efforts to curtail the global reach of these groups must be mindful of the five flows that I described earlier. For example, financial support for terrorist groups is a delicate issue. Many of these groups funnel money from dual-use charities. Yet, if this funding is cut off, their economies will simply go underground, leaving the counterterrorism community with the dilemma of separating legal and laundered money in some Middle Eastern countries that deal in cash. Similarly, what does one do about media outlets that may be providing the cultural conditions for terrorist recruitment? Is al-Jazeera an example of freedom of the press in the Arab world, or is it a terrorist organ? What about the free movement of people? Should countries restrict the movement of certain individuals or groups? If so, how do they justify such decisions? These are all debatable questions. Most terrorist groups are so embedded in these global flows that it is extremely difficult to sort out which people, which ideas, which media, which money, and which weapons are terroristic and which are legitimate. Therefore, this process requires serious thought rather than politicized rhetoric, at least during the first phase of united action against terrorism.

15

Uri Lubrani

WE HAVE HEARD SO MUCH about the global scope of terrorism, but perhaps it would be worthwhile to deviate a little and tell you about my own experience. I am not an academic; rather, I have had to deal personally with the dilemmas of counterterrorism.

Recently, my eighteen-year-old granddaughter asked me whether there is such a thing as "good terrorism." We have been discussing terrorism for years in our household, and my family has long known that I am involved in combating it. Following the horrendous September 11 attacks, the United States issued a new list of terrorist groups that it would no longer tolerate, and Hizballah—whose terrorist activities I have experienced firsthand—was not on it. So this young lady asked me whether Hizballah's brand of terrorism was "good." Of course, this was a legitimate question, and it was good to hear Flynt Leverett of the State Department say that Hizballah is, in fact, a terrorist organization of "global reach"—the first time I have heard such a statement from a U.S. government official since September 11. This point should be reiterated loudly and made official with regard to both Hizballah and Hamas.

As I look at my own encounters with terrorist activities, I divide them into two periods. First came those following the Six Day War, when it became clear to Arab countries that Israel was not to be done in by war. Consequently, the Palestinian constituency decided to resort to violence, and Israelis faced terrorism in many shapes and forms. This, however, did not yet constitute terrorism of global reach.

The second period followed 1979, when Ayatollah Ruhollah Khomeini came to power in Iran and decided to export the Islamic Revolution. He concluded that this end justified the use of terrorism, and at this point we began to see Hizballah's fingerprints on regional terrorism. For example, Imad Mughniyeh, who was trained by the Palestinians to commit terrorist acts for the Palestinian cause, was among those sent to Tehran to train Iranians to do the same; even now, he is more or less commuting between Tehran and southern Lebanon.

Because it was a large, strong, and rich country with many resources, Iran quickly became the "Comintern" for all sorts of terrorism. It was then that Israelis began to notice a new element in Lebanon: a proxy of Iran with its own objectives aside from those of the Palestinians. Why did Iran choose Lebanon? First, Lebanon was open to almost any kind of foreign pressure. Second, some perspicacious official in Iran saw that the Shi'i community in Lebanon could serve as a base for exporting the revolution. So Iran poured funds into Lebanon for social, health, and military purposes; money was no object to Tehran in its relationship with Hizballah. And this strategy has succeeded up to now.

Once Israelis began to feel the impact of this new element, many in the government realized that they had to find a way to pull Israeli troops out of Lebanon. No one in the government had any notion of annexing southern Lebanon; they simply wanted to pacify that part of the northern front. They also realized that the only way to do so was in an orderly fashion. Events did not proceed accordingly, but an orderly withdrawal was the plan from the start; that is why Israel took so long to initiate the pull-out.

But in 1986, came an event that has haunted me ever since. During an Israeli military operation in southern Lebanon, Ron Arad, an air force navigator, was captured by Amal soldiers. I witnessed this event with my own eyes; I saw one of his comrades being rescued, but Arad went astray and was taken prisoner. His captors then whisked him away to Beirut, where, instead of handing him over to the authorities, the head of the Amal movement put him in the cellar of his own home.

As fate would have it, I was appointed by Prime Minister Yitzhak Rabin as head of the team that would negotiate for missing Israeli soldiers. I knew that we had to find a way to communicate directly with the captors rather than with the government of Lebanon, which was totally inept. After a long search, I established contact with a Shi'i in Africa who agreed to talk to his friends in Beirut about Arad. Many weeks later, we began to negotiate with his captors. To this very day, I torment myself at the thought that we bargained. Even though our government had a political reason, we should not have bargained, because at a certain stage, the head of those militants guarding Arad transferred allegiance to Hizballah and took Arad with him. To the best of our knowledge, Hizballah then handed Arad over to the Iranians, or to the Lebanese component of the Iranian Revolutionary Guard Corps, for the sum of approximately $300,000.

Since then, we do not know what has happened to Ron Arad. Is he alive or dead? Who has him? I tell you this story because it marks the point at which Israelis began to see the global reach of terrorism in negotiations with Tehran, Beirut, and Damascus. The United States experienced this problem when Hizballah held American hostages in Beirut for more than a year at the behest of Iran. Israel was asked to help rescue these hostages, and we hoped that by doing so, we could persuade Iran to hand over Arad as well. Not much has been written about Israel's contribution to the release of these American hostages. We gave our assistance readily, and though we failed to retrieve Ron Arad, I am very proud that we had that opportunity to help free the Americans. Yet, I still ask myself why I spoke softly instead of shouting when we were negotiating for Arad; that was my failure.

By now it should be clear that the terrorism sponsored by Iran is a cancer with offshoots into Lebanon, into the territories bordering Israel, into other Arab states, and into many other countries around the world. For example, a United Nations worker in Bosnia told me that there are dormant Hizballah terrorists in that country awaiting orders to begin operating there. Why? Because someone in Iran may decide that there is a reason for activity of that sort in Bosnia (e.g., as revenge, as a political ploy). Hizballah is a direct agent of those who are currently ruling Iran. I would be appalled if Iran were absolved for its role as the Comintern of international terror. If this takes place, Iran's rulers will continue their mischief, if only to preserve their regime—a task that is becoming increasingly difficult for them, even internally. Hopefully, when Phase II of the campaign against terrorism materializes, something will be done about Iran and other terrorism-sponsoring countries.

Let me be clear: I am not calling on the United States to confront Iran right now, nor am I proposing any violent action. But if change does occur there, the entire Middle East will be transformed. Indeed, if the 72 million Iranian citizens become well inclined to the United States and the rest of the Western world, major changes throughout the region will follow. Such change will not happen overnight, but policymakers should keep the potential in mind. A full 80 percent of Iranian citizens want this to happen. Perhaps if the United States gives them a little encouragement, it will.

16

Patrick Clawson

PRESIDENT GEORGE W. BUSH'S RECENT STATEMENTS about terrorism of "global reach" represent quite a change from previous U.S. approaches to counterterrorism. In the past, administrations emphasized that terrorism was criminal activity, and that the methods used by terrorists—primarily their targeting of innocent civilians—were what made their activities unacceptable, irrespective of the causes for which they claimed to be fighting. Since September 11, however, the United States has regarded both terrorism and counterterrorism as a kind of warfare, largely abandoning the criminal-justice approach.

I would be among the first to argue that America's previous criminal-justice approach to terrorism had many shortcomings. Unfortunately, by jettisoning the strengths of this approach along with its weaknesses, the United States has thrown out the baby with the bathwater. Before I turn to defending the principal strength of this criminal-justice approach, though, let me just cite some of its most significant weaknesses, which I have criticized frequently in my testimony and writings.

First, when one treats terrorism as a crime, one is more likely to focus on the particular individuals who engage in terrorist acts rather than on those who order and organize these acts and train the perpetrators; in other words, on operatives at the lowest level rather than those at the top. Second, the American legal system presumes innocence and contains extraordinary protections that must be overcome before one can establish guilt beyond a reasonable doubt, including strict regulations on what kinds of evidence one can offer. The United States has yet to meet these requirements for proving al-Qaeda's involvement in the September 11 attacks. Often, such requirements entail years of exhaustive searching for evidence that is unnecessary to establishing—pretty clearly—which individuals and groups are guilty of specific terrorist activities. During these investigative lulls, terrorist groups may continue to engage in such activities. America thereby loses the many advantages of acting more swiftly, including the chance to prevent further terrorist acts.

Although I am not great fan of the criminal-justice approach, it does have one great advantage—namely, that it depoliticizes terrorism by emphasizing the unacceptability of the means, irrespective of the terrorists' claimed motivations. Indeed, one can quite reasonably argue that terrorists sully the cause in whose name they claim to act; their attacks impede their cause rather than advance it. Therefore, the United States can call on all people to reject terrorism as a matter of principle, irrespective of their views on the particular cause that the terrorists invoke. By depoliticizing terrorism, America can use counterterrorism efforts as an opportunity for cooperation with governments that disagree with it on most other issues. In contrast, by emphasizing that terrorism is a form of warfare, America forces individuals and governments to take sides.

The United States first turned to the criminal-justice approach in part because other governments were hesitant to respond to terrorist acts committed by individuals claiming to represent the Palestinian cause. For example, consider the 1985 incident in which a group of Palestinians hijacked the Italian cruise ship *Achille Lauro* and killed an American passenger. At one point, as the hijackers were fleeing, their plane was intercepted by American fighter jets and forced to land in Italy. Although the Italian government eventually tried and convicted the four hijackers, it released Abu Abbas, the mastermind behind the operation and then-member of the Palestine Liberation Organization's executive committee. Obviously, the Italians felt that holding Abbas or turning him over to the United States would have had too many political ramifications; it would have required them to take a stand on the Palestinian issue, which they did not wish to do. Furthermore, three of the four convicted hijackers have since escaped Italian custody, raising further questions about Italy's political motivations.

Yet, when terrorism is defined as an unacceptable means, irrespective of the end, one frees oneself from such political games, and counterterrorism becomes a matter of police cooperation. Thus, even governments such as Iran or Iraq—which disagree with the United States on many foreign policy issues—may be prepared to agree that terrorism is an unacceptable criminal activity. Indeed, America has had tremendous success over the last fifteen years in persuading not only European and Asian countries but also the Arab League nations to define terrorism as a crime, irrespective of motivation.

Yet, it is this persuasive power that the Bush administration has jettisoned by focusing solely on terrorism of "global reach," implying that there are other kinds of terrorism that the United States will more or less ignore for the time being, particularly the kinds that are specific to a given local conflict. This new approach is not only unprincipled, but also impractical, for four major reasons. First, when the administration says that certain kinds of terrorism need not be addressed immediately, it opens the door to governments that would characterize terrorism against the United States as an understandable political stance, invoking the sympathies of their citizenry to explain why they cannot cooperate in pursuing such terrorists.

Second, this approach forces America to say to other governments, in President Bush's words, "You're either with us, or you're against us." In effect, he is telling these governments that they have to sign on, implicitly, to U.S. foreign policy—that they have to support globalization and U.S. values in order to join the counterterrorism struggle. This is an extraordinarily difficult demand for many governments around the world to stomach. It would be much easier for the president to tell these regimes that they can be completely opposed to every aspect of American foreign policy and society—even regard America as fundamentally evil—and yet still agree that the act of targeting innocent civilians is criminal and impermissible, and that cooperation against terrorists is thus worthwhile. Instead, the administration's new approach will likely narrow its list of potential coalition partners.

Third, by targeting terrorism of "global reach," the United States has set an extraordinarily difficult goal for itself: that of single-handedly solving the problem of terrorism in countries around the world, many of which would not welcome U.S. interference in domestic affairs. The sole criterion for success will be whether or not America puts a complete stop to the activities of these terrorist groups. The previous U.S. approach was quite different. It held that terrorism is a crime; that America would respond to criminal activity occurring on American soil; that America reserves the right to respond to criminal activity against American citizens abroad as well, if the governments in question do not have the means or the will to do so themselves; and that America would stand ready to help any other government wishing to respond to terrorism against its own citizens. This approach delineated much more carefully which sorts of activities the United States would engage in as part of its counterterrorism efforts. It did not require America to eliminate the terrorism of the Sikhs in India or the Corsican separatists in France, or to engage in any other undue interference in the activities of other governments.

Fourth, the very category of "global reach" is of questionable value. Even the most domestic of terrorist groups—those that seem to be focused entirely on specific conflicts within individual countries—often engage in global activities. For example, the groups fighting for an independent Sikh area in India would seem to fit the definition of terrorism that is entirely confined to one country. Yet, these groups have been blamed for the worst case of airplane terrorism prior to September 11. On June 23, 1985, Air India Flight 182 from Canada to New Delhi exploded off the coast of Ireland before a scheduled stop in London, killing all 329 people aboard, including 22 Americans, 160 Canadians, and more than 100 Indian nationals. On that same day, a bag offloaded from a second Canadian flight and bound for another Air India flight exploded prematurely at Tokyo's Narita Airport, killing two airport employees. Sikh militants based in Canada were charged with responsibility for both explosions. Thus, even the most local of terrorist groups tend to have international connections.

Similarly, the Irish Republican Army has received money from Libya and was recently found providing assistance to Colombian terrorists. The fact is, almost all terrorists have engaged in activities that could be defined as being of "global reach." Therefore, this category does not provide boundaries for the U.S. campaign against terrorism, and instead expands America's goals to the point of impracticality, abandoning the principled territory on which it previously stood.

17

Discussion

Richard Abramson, *The Washington Institute:* Can you elaborate on the definition of "global reach"? You have thoroughly documented the global reach of Hizballah, but do you think that this definition will be easy to apply to other terrorist groups?

Patrick Clawson: No—it is an absurd, unprincipled category, and we should reject it out of hand. It is unhelpful to U.S. foreign policy, and is even a significant step backward. Inevitably, it defines groups with "global reach" as those that target the United States, ignoring those that target other countries. Moreover, I cannot think of a single, significant terrorist group that does not have global reach. As the victims of these groups will attest, the various criteria for "global reach" that have been offered by the Bush administration apply to every terrorist organization that the U.S. government has identified worldwide over the last several years. This category is completely unnecessary given the previously careful way that the United States had worked to define terrorism as a violation of principle, an unacceptable means, regardless of its reach. Again, the notion that "global reach" somehow defines and limits the campaign against terrorism is simply wrong. Even the previous strategy of viewing terrorism as a crime was more effective in determining whom the United States should pursue.

Mamoun Fandy: I do not differ much with Patrick on this question. The "global reach" category is another product of the fascination with globalization in general. Many are committed to fighting the "IBMs" of terror, but somehow the local retail shop is not of interest to them. This is not a very useful strategy because it is the local retail shops that are exporting the idea of terrorism on a global scale. All of the formerly local terrorist organizations merit closer examination. Why were they driven out of places like Egypt and Saudi Arabia? How did they move across national boundaries? How did Shaykh

Omar Abdul Rahman move from Asiut University in Egypt to New York? That journey is very important, at both ends. Focusing on a terrorist megaorganization like al-Qaeda while ignoring smaller terrorist groups is terribly misguided.

Uri Lubrani: I agree entirely.

Participant: The 1980s saw the peak of Iranian-inspired terrorism, yet neither the Iranians nor Hizballah tried to stage attacks on U.S. soil during this period. Why do you think this was the case? Second, why do you think Osama bin Laden has never tried to attack Israel?

Lubrani: First of all, the Iranians are clever, and they do not want to take on the United States frontally. Moreover, they had no need to target the United States itself when they could hit American targets overseas, attacking American Marines and the embassy in Beirut. I am not saying that Iranian-backed terrorists will never strike the United States directly. I deem it extremely unlikely, though, because the Iranians are quite attuned to their position in the international community. They are not bin Ladens; they are much more sophisticated in sponsoring terror, doing what they felt they had to do in Germany, France, Argentina, and Beirut. They will continue these activities as long as the current leaders are in power.

As for bin Laden and Israel, let me just say that I have my own suspicions about his activities in that arena, but no proof as of yet. I am still waiting for confirmation of a connection between bin Laden, al-Qaeda, and Imad Mughniyeh, the Hizballah mastermind who has played a part in many terrorist operations against Israelis.

Participant: Uri, you mentioned Damascus during your description of the Ron Arad case. Would you care to elaborate on Syria's possible involvement in terrorism of global reach?

Lubrani: Syria is a terrorism-supporting country by all counts, and is on the U.S. State Department's list of state sponsors. Out of the nearly thirty organizations listed by the United States as being involved in terror, seven are still being hosted by the Syrians. Given this fact, Syria's recent appointment to the United Nations Security Council is completely inexplicable; it is another example of the surrealistic developments that can occur in international politics.

I have not seen any indications that the Syrians will go out of their way to help, or even declare their support for, the United States in its fight against bin Laden, al-Qaeda, and the Taliban. In fact, I know of at least one recent Syrian broadcast that contained a diatribe against the United States. One thing is clear: the Syrians are confused. They do not know which way to move, and there is no unequivocal support among them for the elimination of terrorism—even terrorism within Syria itself.

Participant: Mamoun, to what extent do you think Saudi Arabia has been, as the *New York Times* recently alleged, a willing participant in the rise of Osama bin Laden and al-Qaeda? And in discussing the concept of "global reach," were you arguing that the term itself has been divorced from the strategy that was devised by al-Qaeda for September 11?

Fandy: "Global reach" still needs to be defined very carefully. For instance, local Egyptian terrorists may attack villages in Egypt or kill tourists at Luxor, but the last time I looked, Luxor was part of the globe. That is, localized activities—those that happen "somewhere else"—have to be part of what the United States regards as global if it is serious about rooting out terrorism, building coalitions, sharing intelligence, and so forth.

As for Saudi Arabia, one sound principle holds that most regimes are not interested in the business of self-destruction. On that basis, I do not think that the leaders of Saudi Arabia are interested in flirting with Osama bin Laden and his cohorts. Yet, as a country that considers itself the seat of the Muslim world, Saudi Arabia has long felt compelled to patronize various charitable organizations in the region. Are all of these charitable organizations legitimate? Probably not, but the Saudis sometimes throw money around without tracking what it is used for afterward. Should they be held accountable for terrorist attacks funded by charities that they blindly built in Chechnya, Bosnia, and other countries? Yes, they should learn to be more careful with their money, but I would not be willing to incriminate them at this point.

Participant: I think we can all agree with Patrick that the only reason a given terrorist group might not be of "global reach" is that they have not yet acquired a travel budget. So yes, it is a useless category. Yet, there are other definitional problems with the campaign against terrorism. How will the United States define "innocent civilians"? How will it treat the problem of extradition? For example, the Bush administration has demanded that the Taliban extradite bin Laden. Yet, what if the Northern Ireland peace process falls apart, and Irish Americans start funneling money to the Irish Republican Army (IRA), as they have in the past? My mother gave money to the IRA every year of her life. Were she still alive, could Tony Blair demand her extradition? Similarly, what if an Israeli decides to walk into a mosque and gun down Palestinians—as Baruch Goldstein did in 1994—and some of the victims turn out to be U.S. citizens? Would the United States demand extradition? There are many problematic issues that, understandably, have gone unexamined in the somber days since September 11. I am glad that Patrick, at least, is getting deeply into them.

Karim Haggag, *Egyptian embassy:* I agree. If the United States is going to pile other agendas onto its war against terrorism, how can it justify focusing solely on a country like Iran or an organization like Hizballah? After all, Arab countries will likely say, "Why not add the IRA to the war against terrorism, or Jewish terrorist organizations like Kach and Kahane Chai?" Where does one draw the lines in the U.S. campaign?

Clawson: Karim, your examples are excellent. The United States did go after the IRA and Kach. Back when terrorism was regarded as a criminal matter, the United States mobilized all of its efforts toward halting any activities on U.S. soil that promoted terrorism anywhere in the world, and the Bush administration should resume those efforts. Again, America should adhere to the clear principle that it is willing to go after any kind of terrorism whatsoever, either on its own accord or at the behest of other governments. That is the only way to approach a group like Hizballah, for instance; we must say to them, "If you get out of the terrorism business, we will stop going after you. You can still call for the destruction of Israel and the disappearance of the Jews from the Middle East, but if you don't target innocent civilians, we're not going to regard you as terrorists. We may regard you as a despicable political organization, but we're not going to pursue you with our counterterrorism efforts or ask others to do so." As Ibrahim Karawan said earlier, there is a major difference between someone who expresses disagreement by writing a book and someone who expresses it by waving a machine gun. It is the disagreement by machine gun that characterizes terrorism, not the political objectives of the individuals who perpetrate it.

Granted, there are many terrorist activities that the United States will not get involved in combating of its own accord. Yet, if other governments want U.S. assistance, America will provide it. For example, the United States may at some point help the Indian government with the Sikhs, or the Sri Lankan government with the Tamil Tigers. A doctor in the United States provides most of the funding for the latter group, so the U.S. government could certainly go after him.

Despite the problems with the term "global reach," though, I do not feel that it was employed simply to excuse America from taking action against terrorism occurring in Israel. Yes, that would be one way of reading what the Bush administration has done since September 11. It would be an uncharitable reading, however. I have had just enough experience as a government bureaucrat to know that administrations often do bad things by mistake, not necessarily through malice. Yet, the president and his advisors should not be surprised if some people, especially in Israel, interpret their recent actions in a negative manner. Once they begin using the term "global reach" and omitting certain terrorist groups from the counterterrorism campaign, they will be offending those—often U.S. allies—who are targeted by these groups. This is one of the major shortcomings of the term, along with the fact that it does nothing to narrow the scope of the war on terrorism or to preserve post–September 11 coalitions.

As for Saudi Arabia, I happen to think that many Saudis view Osama bin Laden in much the same way that ordinary Catholics view monks: simply as more devout practitioners of their own beliefs. Altogether too many Saudis accept bin Laden in this manner.

Although I fault the Saudi government for not vigorously combating this viewpoint, I know that it would be very difficult for them to do so. There is a division in Saudi Arabia, dating back to the deal made between the clergy and the government—that the government stays out of education, charitable activities, and religion, and the clerics stay out of defense and oil policy. This would be a very difficult agreement to alter.

PART SIX

Weapons of Mass Destruction in
and from the Middle East:
Challenges for U.S. Policy

18

Judith Miller

W<small>E HAVE HEARD IT SAID</small> repeatedly that the events of September 11 changed everything. I have my doubts about that broad assumption, but I do know that September 11 has changed the way in which we think about terrorist organizations like al-Qaeda and about weapons of mass destruction (WMD).

The personal impact of September 11 was certainly powerful, particularly for those of us in New York. At the time of the attacks, I was near the World Trade Center, voting in the New York primary elections. I came out just in time to see the first tower go up in smoke; it seemed to be sliced in half. We have all seen the pictures, but when you are standing about fifteen blocks from such a disaster, it looks very different. I still worry about the divide between those who were in New York at the time and those who were not.

Although I am a veteran terrorism watcher—experiencing it first-hand in Beirut in 1983, in Cairo soon afterward, and in Paris in 1986—I had never anticipated such attacks in America. Moreover, before September 11, I would not have characterized a jet airliner filled with fuel as a weapon of mass destruction. Yet, this was the terrible brilliance and creativity—if I may be forgiven for using such terms—behind the September 11 attacks: this transformation of a mundane part of American life into a symbol of terror. It was a stroke of innovation that even I, having watched al-Qaeda since 1995, never anticipated.

A little humility is therefore in order for all of us supposed experts on terrorism. September 11 showed us that terrorists do not need an unconventional weapon to stage an unconventional mass attack. It also demolished our traditional profile of the mass terrorist. No longer can we type such a terrorist as a ruthless young man who would be deterred if only he had a job and a wife and some hope for the future of his society. The only thing I would dare to say about the profile of al-Qaeda at this point is that the group has not yet used a woman, and even this fact may eventually prove useless to profilers. Although I doubt that a woman would ever be accepted into the leadership of such an organization, we may see women involved in future terrorist attacks; al-Qaeda has proven itself flexible in the past, and not bound by ideology or doctrine.

Our calculations about the probability of mass terror have also changed since September 11 and the subsequent anthrax attacks. When I was writing *Germs: Biological Weapons and America's Secret War* (2001), the experts in the field told me that I was making too much of biological weapons. One scholar told me that the probability of such weapons being used in the United States was about as great as that of finding oneself on a hijacked airliner. Of course, because I have made so many mistakes myself, I did not put his name in the book. Yet, this was a common notion in the United States: that WMD were unlikely to be used anywhere, and that if they were used, they would be used elsewhere. This notion was based on the assumption that unconventional weapons were largely in the hands of states, and that states understood the consequences of using them. The few exceptions to this rule—isolated and largely ineffective uses of crude chemical and biological agents in the United States—were treated as criminal activities, and nobody regarded them as national security concerns.

Now, though, the U.S. government is beginning to make real changes in the way that it approaches WMD. Before September 11, chemical and biological weapons were regarded as a single WMD subcategory, with biological weapons occupying the caboose of the WMD train. In the world of analysts, real men worried about "nukes." Those men who were not quite senior analysts worried about chemical weapons, while the female analysts worried about biological weapons. The assumption was that "the best and the brightest" did not waste their time focusing on the latter.

The government's assessment of who has WMD has also been altered. In the past, the list of the "dirty dozen" states possessing WMD was published every year and treated as fairly routine. The presence of so many Middle Eastern members in this club—Iraq, Iran, Syria, Libya, and even Israel—has always been disturbing to those who care about a peaceful, stable future in that region. Yet, most people felt that these weapons would remain in the hands of these states.

Although the United States has known since 1993 that al-Qaeda has been seeking WMD capabilities, it was not until a couple of years ago that analysts began to worry about a specific threat: a camp in Afghanistan that contained—according to satellite images—test ranges for various kinds of chemical and biological weapons. In effect, then, al-Qaeda had already entered what is called the "R&D" stage of such weaponry; they had developed crude agents on their own and were testing them on animals. The question of whether the recent anthrax attacks in the United States are connected to al-Qaeda is still unanswered; I have heard excellent arguments on both sides. Should this connection be proven, however, the attacks could clearly be seen as al-Qaeda's entry into the "T&E" stage—that is, the testing and evaluation of such agents to determine their effectiveness at killing people and spreading panic. The United States should not rush to judgment, though, because coming to the wrong conclusion in such matters is dangerous.

Finally, I would like to think that, in light of recent events, the United States will improve its ability to handle any future chemical or biological attacks within its borders. The entire country can do a great deal to prepare for these sorts of attacks. Such preparation is essential, because the appropriate responses to a chemical attack are often inappropriate for a biological attack, and the correct responses to both often run counter to one's instincts.

For example, when I opened a letter at the *New York Times* containing what I thought was anthrax, my colleagues rushed over to me. This was a mistake; everyone should have stayed away. Then, I was taken to the medical department on another floor. Another mistake—had I been contaminated, I might have spread anthrax spores all along the corridor of the newsroom and up to the medical floor. I knew what the appropriate response was, having written about it in my own books, but when this happened to me, I completely forgot about appropriateness and focused on getting the powder off of me and getting myself someplace where I could be treated if, in fact, the worst were true.

Had someone delivered a chemical agent to our newsroom, the response protocol would have been very different. For example, we would have wanted to get everyone out of the newsroom and surrounding areas, not just away from me. We also would have wanted to open nearby windows for ventilation, which would not have been appropriate with some biological agents. Unfortunately, most Americans are completely ignorant about what to do in such situations.

New Yorkers are blessed with the best public health system in the country, the best surveillance system, and some of the best-trained doctors, due in part to the Clinton administration's nationwide improvement efforts, and also to Mayor Rudolph Giuliani's determination after the 1993 World Trade Center attack that New York would be prepared the next time around. Even so, there is much more that can be done, particularly at the national level. The Bush administration is beginning to intensify and accelerate these efforts, but America is a long way from true preparedness. I was greatly distressed, therefore, to see Health and Human Services Secretary Tommy Thompson—someone I greatly admire—appear on *60 Minutes* on September 30, 2001, telling viewers that the United States is already prepared, even though almost everyone, including himself, knew that this was not the case.

The United States must learn from the current attacks in order to prepare. Although very little is known about the anthrax that was used in these attacks, the investigation has found that the agent was not genetically modified. Any anthrax used in the future might well be modified since it has become standard to alter agents in order to make them more lethal or resistant to antibiotics. Civil defense preparations for biological attacks are the obligation of any government that claims to care about its people. If there is a silver lining, of sorts, to the recent attacks, it is that they give Americans an opportunity to pressure their government into spending the funds needed for that preparation.

19

Leon Fuerth

THE SEPTEMBER 11 ATTACKS have illustrated that there is no limit to the violence that some would bring to bear on the United States. Terrorism used to be a retail operation, but it is moving rapidly toward wholesale; the U.S. government must now assume that if terrorists acquired weapons of mass destruction (WMD), they would use them. This constitutes a quantum leap in the threat against the United States, which logically raises the question of whether there should be a quantum leap in the U.S. response. If the answer is "yes," then we are left with the difficult task of defining that response.

Obviously, the Middle East is an area of concern, since several governments there already have—or are trying to acquire—WMD. The most worrisome of these countries are Iraq, Iran, and Syria. Egypt and Saudi Arabia merit attention as well in light of their attempts to acquire ballistic missiles. The Saudis have bought them from China on more than one occasion. These missiles are rather old now, but the Chinese may have a new and improved model to sell. The United States must also pay respectful attention to Israel's WMD capabilities, though the Israelis do not intend to be the first to use such weapons or to introduce new ones into the region.

Although states may well use these weapons in formal military strikes against each other, terrorist groups seem to present a more immediate WMD threat. Consider the 1995 chemical attack on the Tokyo subway system, in which twelve people were killed and more than 5,000 injured. Frighteningly enough, the fatality rate would have been much higher if the Japanese terrorists had been better prepared. The effectiveness of chemical weapons depends on a number of controllable factors: what kind of chemical agents are used; where they are released; whether the release mechanism is designed to attain the right level of dispersion; and whether the agent will persist after release, in such a way that the second wave of victims consists of those who arrive on the scene to help, as happened in New York on September 11. Thus, appropriate response protocols must be devised for different kinds of attacks.

As for biological weapons, the most viable agents include not only anthrax, which has a long storage life, but also smallpox. Years ago, the United States decided to discontinue smallpox vaccinations because smallpox no longer existed as a widespread, naturally occurring disease. Yet, it certainly continues to exist in some laboratory facilities, because no decision was made to destroy the last samples. Even if all of the samples were destroyed, however, technology has reached a point at which a biological agent can be reassembled genetically. Now that most Americans have no resistance to smallpox, should they be concerned by the fact that there are no standby production facilities in the United States for emergency vaccines? America has the means of quickly identifying almost any biological agent used in an attack against it, and yet no capacity to quickly manufacture significant quantities of the vaccines necessary to respond to these agents.

Many other biological weapons have been developed, but they are difficult to handle and require specialized storage facilities. A terrorist would need an agent that has a small signature and that can be developed in small batches, concealed, and transported.

Radiological attacks are a cause for concern as well. For example, placing a jacket of highly radioactive isotopes around even a moderate amount of explosives could contaminate a large target area, or—depending on the half-life of the substance—require a more-or-less permanent resettlement of the population. Similarly, another aircraft attack like that of September 11 could turn a nuclear power plant into a weapon. Such a crash would probably not cause an explosion, but it could trigger a meltdown and a release of radioactive debris. U.S. reactors are surrounded by extremely strong shells of steel and reinforced concrete; even so, any measure taken to guard against such an attack is a measure well taken. Elsewhere in the world, many reactors have no containment shells. For example, there are fifty or more reactors throughout Russia that are akin to the Chernobyl reactor, which had no shell whatsoever.

The changing availability of WMD is another area of concern. In the past, the United States could focus on a handful of more advanced countries serving as the primary sources of WMD technologies and materials for smaller countries in their region, whether it was the Russians leaking materials to Iraq and Iran or the Chinese leaking materials to the Pakistanis. Although these sources remain a problem, the unfortunate fact is that a number of so-called "rogue regimes" have reached a level of sophistication that allows them to swap technologies with each other; along with some of the above-named countries, this group includes North Korea.

Thus, the genie is already partially out of the bottle. Some countries are facilitating the process of WMD development by following the blueprint of regimes that have already been down that road. Yet, information also passes back and forth among much poorer, much less developed countries. An unfortunately large amount of information about WMD is available in the public domain, easily accessible to terrorists.

The United States has been confronted by an adaptive enemy. Thus, Americans must take care not to devote so much attention to closing the door used on September 11 that they leave other doors ajar. Those who planned or supported the recent attacks are likely observing America's reaction and looking for new blind spots to target. My concern is that U.S. efforts to seal off the security breaches that led to September 11 may come at the expense—in both time and resources—of the necessary search for other avenues of attack.

Thus, the Bush administration must deal with a number of rather obvious foreign policy issues that relate directly to the WMD threat. For example, was it wise to dismiss the Comprehensive Test Ban Treaty or the additional verification protocol for the Biological Weapons Convention? Will the United States provide the funding needed to implement its agreement with Russia for the disposal of fifty tons of plutonium? The administration's answer to this latter question is unclear, and part of the money that was returned in the recent tax cut may include funds that would have been used to eliminate this hazardous material. Similarly, will the United States continue its program of buying Russia's highly enriched uranium and converting it into reactor fuel? So far, this program has converted some five thousand former Soviet warheads into fuel for U.S. reactors, but the administration is now taking a second look at it; hopefully, the president will decide to continue the program. Finally, will the United States continue facilitating the elimination of chemical weapons in

Russia? The Russians cannot afford to dispose of these weapons themselves, so the U.S. government must either provide the funding necessary to eliminate this stockpile expeditiously or get used to the idea of it sitting around for the next 200 years.

The question of missile defense is also relevant to WMD discussions. The United States may now have a new opportunity to forge a creative, cooperative solution to this controversial issue; however, I am not sure that this solution should involve abrogating the Anti–Ballistic Missile Treaty. In any case, the United States certainly needs to proceed at top speed on the development and deployment of theater missile defense, in part to help its allies in the Middle East, including Israel.

Some WMD issues involve more than just the question of funding. For example, America has unfinished business with Iraq, and the question is whether now is the time to finish that business. The Bush administration has basically denounced the existing UN sanctions against Iraq and proposed new "smart sanctions" designed to put any Iraqi WMD capabilities under tighter guard. Unfortunately, France and Russia teamed up in the UN Security Council to veto these new sanctions, leaving the ineffective remnants of the old sanctions and greater unease about what is going on in Iraq. Will the Bush administration abandon the quest for smart sanctions and switch back to smart bombs? If so, when? Of course, if a credible link is established between the current anthrax attacks and Iraq, this switch might occur rather soon.

Similarly, what will happen to U.S. relations with the Chinese if the latter do not fully honor their commitments regarding nonexport of chemical and nuclear materials to places like Pakistan? What about the U.S. relationship with Russia? The one that the Clinton administration tried to build nearly self-destructed over efforts to stop the Russians from exporting technology that was aiding Iranian development of intercontinental ballistic missiles and WMD capabilities. Now that the United States seems to have begun a new romance with Russia, how far will the Bush administration go to preserve the relationship if these exports persist?

In general, it may be helpful to think of the U.S. campaign against WMD proliferation as a clock, of sorts. At one o'clock is counterproliferation, a stage in which the administration simply decides what it would do if a particular country acquired WMD. At three o'clock is one possible response to this eventuality: deterrence. At six o'clock is consequence management; that is, preparing America for any possible WMD attack. At eight o'clock is retaliation: deciding what sort of action the United States would take against the perpetrators of such an attack, and whether or not such action should be bound by the rules of proportional response.

Finally, sometime after eight o'clock is preemption, an option that has not been on the table for quite a while. Is the administration prepared, for example, to simply watch as an unfriendly regime acquires WMD capabilities, with the United States relying only on diplomacy or defensive technologies? Or should America use its capacity to forcibly eliminate such capabilities? This option may sound extreme, but as I said earlier, there is no longer an upper threshold to the amount of violence that some would bring to bear against the United States. In the case of WMD, America faces a threat to its very existence, so it is time to put all of the options back on the table and reexamine them.

The current campaign against terrorism may require some rethinking as well. Personally, I am not entirely satisfied with the administration's definition of this campaign. Is it possible to wage an effective war against terrorism of "global reach" while ignoring local terrorism? Probably not, particularly if the United States is looking to enlist the cooperation of those who are suffering from the latter variety. The range of the administration's intentions is unclear at the moment, but a broad scope will be of the utmost importance later on. Beyond Afghanistan, the administration must focus on destroying the unique quality of contemporary terrorism that gives it the means to threaten America: the fact that it is networked. By doing so, the United States should be able to segment terrorism into smaller units that can be dealt with more effectively on a local basis.

What are the elements of the terrorism network? One is privacy of communications; terrorists can now obtain high-grade, commercially available encryption technology. Another is freedom of travel; terrorists can find sanctuary in many countries and take refuge behind international borders.

What methods, then, are required to eliminate such a network? One possibility is massive surveillance, which citizens of liberal democracies may find very difficult to absorb. A second possibility is the forcible removal of terrorists from the sovereign territory of other countries. Other options include preemption and acts of sabotage. All of these possibilities go to the heart of America's culture of legality and approach to ethics. For example, should U.S. officials issue subpoenas for terrorists to appear in federal court, or should they deal with such individuals in a more forceful, perhaps even permanent, fashion? Terrorist networks directly and physically challenge the very continuity of the United States, and Americans must therefore reexamine the envelope of acceptable action and decisionmaking regarding these networks.

20

Discussion

Dennis B. Ross, *The Washington Institute:* I would like to shape the discussion a bit, because there seems to be a clear bifurcation here. On the one hand, there is the question of threat: which threat should concern us the most, and which threats will arise in the near future. On the other hand is the question of response, and Leon did an excellent job of categorizing the potential responses to weapons-of-mass-destruction (WMD) proliferation: moral suasion, collective international protocols, deterrence, and even strategies based on the notion that the best defense is a good offense. One point common to both presentations is that any limitations on the threats we faced before September 11 no longer exist.

I will begin with two questions of my own for both panelists, concerning the WMD threat from terrorist groups. One popular view is that if al-Qaeda actually possessed WMD, they would have already used these weapons. Do you agree with this assumption? Second, do you think that terrorist groups would or could seek help on WMD development from any of the states that you identified as being capable of providing such assistance?

Judith Miller: Again, there is evidence that al-Qaeda has developed rudimentary biological and chemical capabilities. Many analysts in the Federal Bureau of Investigation and the Bush administration place the group at the early trial stage, in which they would be testing agents that they have already developed. I am not entirely convinced by such assumptions, but I am sure that if al-Qaeda had a weapon that its leaders thought was workable, they would use it.

From this point of view, al-Qaeda's intense interest in crop dusters becomes deeply disturbing. Fortunately, crop dusters are an extremely difficult means of disseminating biological agents, requiring many special adjustments. The Iraqis worked long and hard at trying to figure out how to use crop dusters in this manner. Initially, they had only limited success, but then the United Nations inspectors were forced to leave Iraq, and analysts were no longer able to monitor their capability in this area.

Aside from Iraq, al-Qaeda might be more likely to recruit an individual rather than a state for help on biological weapons, such as a Soviet scientist who had worked on WMD, someone from the South African WMD program, or even an American expert. In the latter case, they would have to be satisfied with a very old American, because the United States has not had an offensive biological weapons program since 1969. Such talent is out there, though, which is why the Clinton administration was wise to seek productive employment for, and cooperation between, thousands of former WMD experts in the United States and former Soviet Union. These cooperative threat reduction programs have been much underappreciated, however, and Congress has cut their funding bit by bit since their inception. Yes, the Russians have been difficult to work with on such endeavors; they have kept their military facilities tightly closed, and many Americans felt that by helping Russian civilian scientists, the United States might in effect be helping the Russian military program. Yet, for many such scientists, the only alternative to participating in U.S. threat reduction programs is to work for a country like Iran. This is the danger of cutting these programs—for years, the Iranian government has conducted recruiting missions in former biological weapons facilities in Russia, enticing Russian scientists to work in Iran.

So to answer your question, yes, if al-Qaeda had workable WMD, it would use them. I do not know whether the post–September 11 anthrax attacks were perpetrated by al-Qaeda, but we cannot exclude that possibility. Moreover, we should worry less about state sponsorship of terrorist WMD development than about individuals; it is individuals, and the expertise that travels with them, that pose the greatest danger.

Leon Fuerth: I agree with Judith and would argue that the best way to disrupt WMD proliferation is to deny terrorist groups the time and facilities required to develop such weapons. Al-Qaeda has managed to find sufficient time and sanctuary in the past, and if they are not contained, they will eventually possess viable WMD. Typically, the United States is reactive when confronted by an enemy like al-Qaeda, largely because there has long been an envelope of permissible options for dealing with such groups. This envelope does not often change through simple foresight. Events change it—specifically, catastrophic events. For example, before September 11, analysts could have talked about the need for homeland defense until they were blue in the face, but no significant measures would have been implemented until after the attacks occurred. Al-Qaeda is an imaginative enemy, though, and if the United States remains in its reactive mode—that is, responding only to demonstrated threats—then WMD will eventually be employed against an American target.

Participant: I would like to ask the panelists a question on the issue of response. Both of you indicated quite clearly that the U.S. government has not dealt with various WMD issues in a proactive way, partly because other priorities are on the agenda. Could you offer some prescriptions on how the media and others can help to galvanize both the government and the public into being more proactive about such issues? Where does one draw the line between panicking and informing Americans, so that public opinion drives the government to take action?

Fuerth: The media's interest in a subject persists as long as the subject is hot. After that, the media reverts to being reactive. If the public's best hope of staying abreast of WMD issues is through print or television news stories, how much hope can there be when the media periodically abandons certain topics in favor of new ones that will grab a larger audience share? For example, will the media still be following through on the anthrax story a year from now if no further incidents have occurred in the interim? Or will it fall back into reactive mode, where it is left wondering what happened when a similar catastrophe arises? The media has a responsibility to make weighty decisions in this area. Instead of babbling on repetitively about the circumstances of the anthrax attacks, for example, the press could investigate and report on adequate systems of response to such attacks—that is, offer working details on such systems in order to give the public information upon which to base its demands.

Congress has a similar tendency toward amnesia. Fortunately, representative government does work—if the public applies enough pressure, members of Congress will begin to understand that their response to all of the above concerns will affect their political future. If Americans do not make it clear that WMD issues are meaningful to them, however, then it may take another catastrophe to spur Congress into taking significant action.

Miller: Certainly, the frenetic pace that news coverage adopted following September 11 cannot continue indefinitely. The key factor is how the media sustains public interest and continues asking the tough questions. For those of us in the newspaper business, there is a barrier between covering the news and making it, between reporting on what a particular senator has to say about WMD and offering our own views. Several factors make it difficult to accomplish the latter. Because of my recent book on biological weapons, I have been given a bit more leeway in this regard than usual—normally, I would not be asked to offer my own solutions and positions so publicly. America is a big country with many different preoccupations, so even the most important of national issues must often share space with local concerns. For example, when I visited Chicago recently, I was surprised to discover that while the events of September 11 and afterward have generated tremendous concern there, they are not quite as overwhelming and all-absorbing for residents of Chicago as they have been for residents of New York and Washington. I suspect that the same difference holds in other parts of the country as well. Thus, keeping a large public wholly focused on one issue, however important, can be a real challenge.

Orna Shulman, *The Washington Institute:* My question concerns preemption, a response option that, as Leon pointed out earlier, has not been used much by the U.S. government of late. The United States has an understandable fear of international condemnation, given the criticism that Israel faced after its 1981 preemptive strike on the nuclear reactor in Osirak, Iraq. Will this attitude change in light of the bits of evidence that seem to point to possible Iraqi involvement in the September 11 attacks and/or the subsequent anthrax attacks? Under the current circumstances, what standards of proof would the U.S. government need before it felt confident that it could take action against Iraq's WMD capabilities without causing an international uproar?

Fuerth: The United States did take a kind of preemptive action relatively recently, when it launched cruise missiles against a purported chemical weapons plant in Sudan in August 1998. That attack was not frivolous—regardless of the surrounding controversy, it was based on evidence that the government had acquired over a long period of time. Of course, there is a difference between legal evidence—information that one could take into court with an expectation of winning a case—and evidence that, while not definitive, tilts the balance in favor of certain conclusions. In my experience, intelligence information is hardly ever clear enough to be decisive, which leaves decisionmakers with the dilemma of concluding for themselves when they are justified in acting and what sort of action is appropriate. Yet, if these leaders defer acting until they get information that meets legal standards, the consequences could be dire.

Ross: Given my own experience with this issue, I would say that preemption has less to do with standards of evidence than with the threshold of fear and the consequences of inaction. If America's attitude changes to a point at which it feels that it must act preemptively on inconclusive evidence in order to protect itself, it would not be swayed much by international criticism. As Leon said, though, it may take yet another catastrophe before the government deems the consequences of inaction too grave and moves from a posture of moral suasion and deterrence to one of preemption and compulsion. Although there is a danger that such changes would lead the United States to operate with a hair trigger, fear—whether generated by September 11 or some future event—may well bring about a world in which America is quick to act preemptively.

Miller: Biological weapons pose unique problems for preemption, though. Nuclear programs are fairly transparent, as we saw with the Osirak facility. Although the International Atomic Energy Agency insisted that this plant was used solely for peaceful power generation purposes, telltale signatures of more sinister activity were evident there, and a case could be assembled in favor of attacking it. But such a case would be almost impossible to make for biological facilities, short of actually entering and inspecting them, because most of them cannot be identified from the outside. American satellites flew over former Soviet facilities for years without resolving the debate about whether they were in fact producing biological weapons. If a facility can make a regular pharmaceutical, then it can make anthrax, and unless one has evidence from inside the plant, there is no way of telling what it is producing.

How can the United States take preemptive action against such facilities? It cannot simply start bombing a suspected country's pharmaceutical industry. That is the special challenge of biological weaponry, which is why I find it strange that any "rogue" country would risk sanctions and preemptive attacks by pursuing nuclear rather than biological weapons.

Raymond Tanter, *University of Michigan:* My question concerns both threat and response. In the wake of September 11, President Bush appointed Richard Clarke to the new post of special advisor for cyberspace security, highlighting concerns that weapons of mass disruption might become as real a threat as weapons of mass destruction. Imagine the added chaos that would have occurred if a cyberterrorist attack had been launched in tandem with the September 11 attacks. How, then, should cyberterrorism factor into U.S. WMD policies?

Fuerth: During my time in the Clinton administration, we tried to develop a system for dealing with the threat of cyberterrorism in cooperation with U.S. private industry. Yet, we were resisted every step of the way, even in our efforts to compile statistical information on the scope of the threat. For example, many individual companies were hesitant to report incidents in which hackers had broken into or disrupted their computer systems, despite the friendly assurances of the U.S. government that such information would be kept in the strictest of confidence. Moreover, U.S. software companies waged a secret war against the administration over the export of high-grade encryption technology, which they felt was their vital edge in an extremely competitive world market. Consequently, both the FBI and the intelligence community found it increasingly difficult to monitor terrorist activities as individuals like Osama bin Laden acquired the means to encrypt their communications.

Unfortunately, future efforts toward improving vigilance will necessarily delve into the stockpile of personal freedoms and privacy that Americans enjoy; this will be one of the toughest challenges in the post–September 11 campaign for homeland security. In his October 7 *New York Times* article entitled "A Watchful State," Jeffrey Rosen—a law professor at George Washington University—addressed this campaign by describing surveillance efforts in Great Britain. In the early 1990s, the British began installing public surveillance systems in response to Irish Republican Army terrorism. Even though such terrorism has long declined, there are still an estimated 2.5 million cameras in place, observing even the most petty of crimes.

The United States could easily establish a similar national system; for example, mailboxes could be wired to record images of anyone who delivers a package, anywhere, anytime. The government may soon be able to obtain this kind of information and make it universally available to all agencies of law enforcement and intelligence. Other feasible measures include the collection of an individual's genetic information and the use of machines that read facial structure and more. Of course, if Americans allow technology to set the pace, they run the risk of creating an Orwellian society. They must therefore find a balance between safeguarding their democratic freedoms and ensuring national security.

Charles Duelfer, *former deputy chairman, UNSCOM:* As both panelists pointed out, there is an important difference between state and nonstate actors when it comes to the use of WMD. The U.S. policy of deterrence has succeeded in keeping other states from using such weapons against it. For example, during the Gulf War, Saddam Husayn was deterred from employing his WMD arsenal because he realized that the United States would obliterate him if he actually did so. Today, however, various nonstate actors are gaining access to such weapons, which enhances the possibility of their being used covertly. Biological weapons, in particular, are difficult to track; for example, a nonstate actor could wreak havoc on the United States by spreading foot-and-mouth disease, yet the government would be hard pressed to link such an epidemic to its causal agent. Thus, there is little to deter nonstate actors from attempting such attacks if they have the capability.

Recognition of this fact inevitably leads me back to preemption as a policy option to which the United States should devote far more attention in the post–September 11 world. Do the panelists have any more ideas about the viability of pursuing preemptive policies in the Middle East? How might the United States structure such policies and sell them to its allies in the region? How can the Bush administration move the various states in the counterterrorism coalition to scrutinize or take action against those of their citizens who would do harm to the United States, with or without WMD?

Fuerth: I do not know the answer to that question, but it must indeed be put out in the open for discussion, if only because the scale of the potential threat to the United States is so great. The American reaction to what took place on September 11 was magnificent, for the most part, but no one really knows how many more such incidents Americans could absorb, either as individuals or as a nation. One thing is sure—most people have accepted as a statistical probability the notion that another major attack will occur. Thus, the United States must at the very least find ways to disrupt the gestation of any such attack.

Bernard Leventhal, *The Washington Institute:* One preventive measure that has been little discussed here is human intelligence. The United States seems to have underfunded—or perhaps simply underdirected—its activities along this line. Should the government devote more funds to the development of human intelligence? Obviously, it is difficult for a Caucasian to penetrate an Arab terrorist cell, but there must be other ways of infiltrating such groups, along with, if need be, the states that directly or indirectly support them.

Fuerth: The culture of the U.S. intelligence community must be transformed, and such changes would require perhaps a decade to take hold. Any new culture will have to be nurtured; in particular, youths must be shown that there are viable careers to be made in the intelligence field. Preparation for such careers must begin relatively early, because it takes a long time to develop the necessary proficiencies (e.g., fluency in the languages of the Middle East). But the government should not hesitate to invest its resources in fostering this sort of intensive, lifelong preparation.

As important as human intelligence is, the United States now has an immediate and unprecedented opportunity to take preemptive action in another crucial area: banking. Most forms of international crime and international terrorism have at least one thing in common: a dependence on international banking systems. Banks have long held themselves to be in a special category, exempt from any sort of systemic change stemming from the illegal activities of individual clients, even if these activities threaten the very nations and economies upon which the banks depend. This exemption may now be ending, though, in part because of UN Security Council Resolution 1373, which was approved unanimously on September 28, 2001. Among other things, this resolution mandates that all member states criminalize the financial activities of terrorist groups like al-Qaeda and freeze their monetary assets. If such measures can force the international banking system to become transparent in this manner, the United States will have a major new weapon against both international crime and international terrorism.

Participant: Shortly after September 11, the new Office of Homeland Security was created, and Tom Ridge—a former congressman and governor—was appointed as its director, a cabinet-level post. This may be a step in the right direction, but how do we ensure that the primary responsibility for responding to all of the issues that we have discussed here does not fall on one cabinet member, or one office? Ideally, shouldn't responsiveness be a shared burden?

Fuerth: Congress should recover some of its responsibility in this area. In place of the countless committees that assert jurisdiction on these issues, though, Congress will need to create a single, joint committee involving both houses and both major parties. Otherwise, those in the government who are wrestling with post–September 11 dilemmas will have to spend an inordinate amount of time testifying to a myriad of related committees and jurisdictions. This single committee must also be granted the decisive word over the allocation of money; this all-important appropriating power can be used to fuse the activities of the administration.

Under the current system, Ridge will run into difficulties as he tries to direct homeland security activities in ways that have monetary consequences. The structure of the intelligence community serves as an instructive example of this problem. George Tenet wears two hats: director of the Central Intelligence Agency (CIA) and head of the overall intelligence community. The CIA is firmly under his control, but the rest of the intelligence community does not necessarily allow him to have full control over its operating revenue.

In contrast, the drug czar found a way to alleviate this problem by demanding some power to affect relevant appropriations before assuming that post. President Bush should support Ridge on similar requests, helping him to create interagency orchestration and obtain the funds that are required for such orchestration. The administration has two means of accomplishing these ends. One is to seek a legislative mandate for Ridge's efforts. This is a slow process, though, and pursuing it now would be premature. Ridge's activities should be phased, beginning with the sorts of experimentation and practical work that can be done with presidential authority, and perhaps later moving toward a congressional mandate. The administration's other option is to work directly through its Office of Management and Budget—that is, to go to the various relevant agencies and convince them in one way or another that cooperating with each other under Ridge's supervision would be in their best interests.

Participant: Creating a new mindset for the post–September 11 world involves rethinking not only the roles of Congress and the Bush administration, but also the public debate about response. September 11 has inspired a level of unity and patriotism among Americans and within Congress that had not been seen in quite a while. At the same time, these sentiments have diluted the public debate about the appropriate response to the attacks, as if any such debate would somehow be unseemly. As wonderful as this unity is, Americans must now foster public debate on the numerous issues that the panelists have raised. How might this debate be conducted in a way that other countries do not view it as a sign of weakness or vacillation? How can the press reassure Americans that now is in fact an appropriate time to debate these issues?

Miller: Newspapers have been quick to take up this debate, with numerous daily articles on the appropriate response to September 11, on the mistakes of previous and current administrations, and so forth. Personally, I am focusing my energies on following the investigation of the perpetrators and covering the most critical issue—namely, how we can ensure that these sorts of attacks do not happen again. Yes, this focus will eventually encompass debates concerning civil liberties and national security, or criticism of previous administrations, or arguments about why the United States was unable to prevent the attacks in the first place. At the moment, though, such debates are not very productive, and perhaps even a bit exasperating.

My concern now is whether Americans have the discipline to prioritize, to focus on the most critical issues. One thing that I learned from studying Osama bin Laden and al-Qaeda is that they believe in one-two punches—that is, in planning their attacks in two waves. Sometimes the second wave is successful, more often it is not. Yet, if a second attack on the United States were to occur now, I dread to think of what might happen to the national psyche.

Americans should therefore not concentrate on truly divisive issues right now. Instead, they should worry about the most urgent matters, such as how they are going to produce the vaccine needed to safeguard U.S. troops against anthrax. The Clinton administration said that it would provide such vaccinations in 1997, only to find, much to its shock and dismay, that it could not; this is the sort of issue that merits immediate attention.

Ross: The debate about long-term response must take place within the Bush administration as well as in public forums. The only way to generate a new mindset in the government is by conducting a post-mortem on September 11—one that examines not only the mistakes that were made by the intelligence community, but also the government's past and present assumptions about where the greatest WMD threats are most likely to arise.

Participant: Judith, since you are one of the most knowledgeable people in the United States about both Iraq and bioterrorism, let me ask you to speculate about the recent anthrax attacks. First, assuming

that al-Qaeda was involved in these attacks—which is by no means a
certainty at this point—to what extent might they have received assistance from Iraq? If they have, in fact, developed a nascent capacity
to produce biological weapons on their own, would this obviate the
need for Iraqi assistance? Second, regardless of their possible involvement in the anthrax attacks, there can be no doubt that the Iraqis
have growing stockpiles of chemical and biological weapons, and that
Saddam Husayn is attempting to acquire nuclear weapons as well.
Based on your assessment of Saddam, do you think that the United
States can rely on deterrence to prevent him from using WMD in
the future?

Miller: We at the *New York Times* have been feverishly investigating
the alleged Iraqi connection to the events of September 11 and afterward, largely because it is becoming a matter of debate within the
administration and the Pentagon. Many at the Pentagon believe that
there is a connection, while others in the intelligence community
and at the State Department argue that there is no real evidence to
substantiate this belief. For example, one of the chief allegations is
that one or more of the September 11 hijackers met with an Iraqi
intelligence agent in Prague months before the attacks, even though
some investigators have been unable to confirm such a meeting. Similar efforts to tie Iraq to the 1993 attack on the World Trade Center
have also failed to produce compelling evidence.

As much as many Americans would like to find a connection
between Iraq and al-Qaeda, the fact is that Saddam Husayn is doing
quite well without having to provide covert backing for attacks against
the United States. He has effectively ended his economic and political isolation. The U.S.-led sanctions are laughable; he can buy
anything he wants. He has even gained the sympathy of the world
for the starving Iraqi children, never mind the fact that they are starving because he uses the country's funds for weapons and palaces rather
than for medicine and food.

As for deterrence, it has been effective in the past—as Charles
Duelfer pointed out, Saddam was warned not to use WMD during
the Gulf War, and he did not use them. Saddam is not crazy—he is a
bully, and he knows his limits. For the most part, I do not see him
posing the threat level that others have assigned to him. The sole

exception is his biological weapons arsenal, which does in fact scare me to death. Again, biological weapons can be delivered with no return address, so he could use them without the United States being able to marshal the kind of intelligence and evidence needed to justify a counterstrike.

Participant: Leon, I would like to hear your insider's perspective on the Clinton administration's policy toward bin Laden and al-Qaeda—a policy for which you, obviously, were not responsible. Specifically, that administration faced several major provocations from these terrorists: the various highly publicized bin Laden *fatwas* calling for the murder of Americans; the well-documented terrorist training camps that he set up in Afghanistan, presumably to prepare thousands of adherents to carry out his *fatwas*; and the 1998 attack on the U.S. embassies in Kenya and Tanzania. The most significant and visible response to these provocations—a cruise-missile attack against one of bin Laden's camps shortly after the embassy bombings—failed to achieve the desired results. Why didn't the Clinton administration do what the Bush administration has done recently—namely, demand that the Taliban extradite bin Laden and his apparatus, and respond to any refusal with a sustained military attack against Afghanistan?

Fuerth: To begin with, there is no evidence that, prior to September 11, the current administration was considering doing anything more about al-Qaeda than the Clinton administration had done. During its first several months in office, the Bush administration likely felt constrained within the same general envelope of possibilities that guided the Clinton administration. That envelope is defined differently now, but it may eventually recede to its pre-September 11 dimensions.

What defined the envelope before September 11? First was the doctrine of proportionality, which held that the United States is not supposed to mete out disproportionate levels of death and destruction, even in the process of self-defense. Hence, America was roundly criticized for the cruise missile attack on Sudan, and even for a Gulf War attack on what intelligence said was a biological warfare plant in Iraq. This factor raises the question of civilian casualties as well. Suppose, for example, that a terrorist training camp is also home to several hundred of the terrorists' dependents. Have we stopped caring whether or not women and children die? As the Clinton administration found out, pinpointing individual targets while trying to avoid unnecessary casualties is difficult, even with reliable intelligence on the ground and cruise missiles ready to fire.

A second potentially limiting factor is the longstanding executive order banning assassination. Calls to overturn this ban were heard well before September 11 and have only grown louder since. Yet, Americans must face the possibility that there are some who would like nothing more than to indict a U.S. president or military leader under an international war crimes tribunal for carrying out assassinations or any of the other policies that I have just mentioned.

A third potential limitation is the question of coalition management. For example, the United States needs Saudi cooperation for airborne missions over northern Iraq. Yet, as the U.S. government pursues newly aggressive policies in the region, the Saudis might decide that they can no longer allow such missions, and the United States would find itself unable to constrain that part of Iraq from the air. The same dilemma arises with Turkey, from which the U.S. military stages another set of air missions into Iraq.

Barbi Weinberg, *The Washington Institute:* First, regarding the preemption of Iraq's potential nuclear capabilities, Israel did the United States a big favor in destroying the Osirak facility. Since then, however, Iraq has apparently disseminated and hidden its nuclear materials throughout the country, in a way that would make them difficult to find. Assuming that the United States could find and destroy these materials, though, would it feel compelled to wait until Iraq was able to actually use them? September 11 has likely made this question easier to answer.

Second, regarding human intelligence, I am not sure that America can wait a decade for improvements. Training young people for careers in intelligence is fine, but the government has to do something much more quickly. The intelligence community is at a disadvantage right now, but it cannot afford to defer change.

Andrew Shapiro, *legislative assistant to Senator Hillary Rodham Clinton:* Judith, what is your impression of the U.S. response to the anthrax

threat thus far? As a congressional staffer, I have been offered conflicting recommendations for dealing with this threat. For example,
the Centers for Disease Control and Prevention (CDC) says that
people in my position should be taking the antibiotic Cipro. Yet,
infectious disease experts have argued against this recommendation
in the *New York Times*, saying that Cipro-takers will develop an im-
munity to the drug and inadvertently help to create an
antibiotic-resistant strain of anthrax.

I therefore get the sense that certain individuals may be recom-
mending Cipro without a real medical basis for doing so, as a
psychological palliative to those who may have been exposed to anthrax. What concerns me most is that if a more serious anthrax attack
occurs, there may not be a single, authoritative voice telling Americans how to respond, and people are liable to become panicked and
confused as a result. Even now, more than a few congressional staff-
ers are trying to get tested for anthrax even though they were nowhere
near the contaminated sites. Is there a way of managing how recommendations are made to the public during this sort of crisis?

Miller: In addition to the conflicting advice about response, Americans are getting mixed messages from the Bush administration about
the anthrax itself. One day they are told that everything is under
control, and the next day they are told that the agent used in the
attacks was pure, highly potent, and weaponized. The day after that,
the administration backpedals: "No, the anthrax wasn't weaponized;
it's simply the Ames strain." In case anyone finds that reassuring, let
it be known that the Ames strain is a very nasty kind of anthrax.
There is no nonpotent strain of anthrax other than the vaccine strains,
which cannot be turned into a weapon.

In terms of advice, the CDC has been terrible; it has neither
issued clear guidelines nor established a single, central source from
which Americans can get the information they need. Moreover, its
initial decision to recommend Cipro is shortsighted. People should
not take this drug unless they absolutely have to; if used extensively
now, Cipro will not be effective when it is truly needed. Several other
drugs could have been prescribed—doxycycline or other tetracyclines,
penicillin—but initially, everyone wanted the extra security blanket
that Cipro was said to provide.

The same sort of confusion and contradiction has been seen in many of the public discussions about smallpox. Certainly, the prospect of a smallpox attack is frightening, and it is true that the general population no longer has resistance to this disease. Yet, it is unfair to criticize the government for halting vaccinations years ago. At the time, smallpox was an eradicated disease. The Department of Health and Human Services had no compelling reason to continue mass vaccinations, particularly when people in the United States and all over the world were dying of AIDS. These tough choices persist, of course—we still have not developed any sort of vaccine for AIDS.

Despite all of the problems with the government's initial response, we must acknowledge that it is difficult to make all of the right choices when dealing with such an unprecedented situation. Moreover, Tom Ridge—with the help of Gen. Wayne Downing, the newly appointed deputy national security advisor for combating terrorism—is beginning to assemble a coherent system for dealing with this sort of crisis. Therefore, I would recommend that Americans show a little patience, while they persist in pressuring the government to continue in these efforts.

PART SEVEN

Antiterror 'Coalitions': Prospects and Problems

21

Roundtable Discussion

GILLES ANDRÉANI	Former director of policy planning, Foreign Ministry, France
MOSHE ARENS	Former foreign and defense minister, Israel
ABDUL RAOUF AL-REEDY	Former Egyptian ambassador to the United States
DENNIS B. ROSS	Former special Middle East coordinator; counselor/Ziegler distinguished fellow, The Washington Institute

MODERATOR: Robert B. Satloff, *executive director, The Washington Institute*

Robert B. Satloff: As the campaign against terrorism unfolds, we must examine the nature of the evolving coalition that will carry it forward. In particular, we must get a sense of how individual governments view this campaign, including its future course and their own role in it. Let me begin very generally, then, by inviting each of the panelists—who are not speaking for their governments, but who can nevertheless offer a great deal of insight into what their governments are thinking—to describe what they see as the objective of the campaign against terrorism. Ambassador al-Reedy?

Abdul Raouf al-Reedy: The attacks against the United States on September 11 were crimes not only against the American people, but also against civilization. No grievance whatsoever—be it religious, political, or ideological—could possibly justify these heinous acts. Those involved should receive the most severe punishment.

Egypt has been victimized by terrorism for years. Our great president Anwar Sadat was a victim, and terrorists have also attempted to assassinate President Hosni Mubarak. The prime minister of Egypt, the speaker of the People's Assembly, and the foremost Egyptian writer

(Naguib Mahfouz, winner of the Nobel Prize for literature) have all been targets of terror. The bombing of the Egyptian embassy in Pakistan and the various attempts to harm the Egyptian tourism industry must also be mentioned on the long list of terrorist attacks that Egypt has suffered. Egypt fought the battle against terrorism by itself, and it was a lonely battle. The perpetrators and planners of these crimes found safe haven not only in Afghanistan, but also in the fashionable residential quarters of Western capitals. There, they had wide access to the media, and were frequently seen giving interviews on television.

Having been victimized by terror ourselves, we Egyptians feel profound shock and grief about September 11. Egypt wholeheartedly sympathizes with the American people. As President George W. Bush pointed out in a recent speech, memorial services were held in Egyptian mosques immediately after the attacks, in sympathy with America.

Today, the world as a whole faces a grave crisis, one that could deeply affect our way of life for some time to come. Egyptians and Americans belong to different cultures and have different perspectives; we may even have divergent interpretations of history. It is our duty as Egyptians, however, to share the perspective that we have gained from our own experience. We owe it to our American friends, for we believe that the coalition against terrorism should achieve maximum success in its mission. That mission is nothing less than the eradication of terrorism from the face of the earth.

Yet, it is absolutely vital to guard against turning the campaign against terrorism into a war between the Muslim world and the West—a war between religions or civilizations. Fortunately, most Western and Muslim leaders are fully aware of that danger and are taking steps to prevent it. But this responsibility does not rest solely with heads of state. This is a war in which ideas, symbols, and words play a significant role. Writers, professors, journalists, and historians must be careful in their communications with one another. It is essential that Western and Muslim intellectuals engage in a dialogue to determine how they can alert their respective societies to this potential danger. Indeed, terrorists are not the only ones who can lead us into religious war. Those espousing extremism on both sides can also, intentionally or unintentionally, push the world into a clash of civilizations.

For many years, we have been asking that the underlying causes of terrorism be addressed. Paramount among these problems is that of the Palestinians. This issue has been with us for almost a century, causing a great deal of havoc in our part of the world and clouding the wonderful relationship that existed for centuries between Jews and Muslims. Nothing has distorted the political climate in the Middle East more than this problem, and it is time that it be resolved on the basis of the universally accepted United Nations (UN) Security Council resolutions and the exchange of land for peace. Nothing serves the cause of the terrorists more than the continuation of the Palestinian problem.

On a daily basis, the Arab and Muslim worlds watch as Palestinian cities are invaded, houses blown up, trees uprooted, and political leaders assassinated. The innocent victims include Israelis as well as Palestinians, and the cycle of violence has taken a heavy toll on both sides. Arab and Muslim youths witness these atrocities on television. They watch with a sense of anger, humiliation, and despair: perfect ingredients for extremism and fanaticism. Therefore, solving the Palestinian problem would deprive the terrorists of a powerful weapon—the cause of Palestine.

This is a challenge that we all must face—Arabs, Israelis, and Americans. The U.S. role is, of course, paramount. President Bush has emphasized that the war on terror will be fought on a number of fronts, but the chronic problem of Palestine should be high on the agenda of the comprehensive struggle. A better world can emerge from these terrible events if we approach the present challenge as a worldwide coalition, determined to safeguard our civilization. It is, after all, a civilization to which peoples from every corner of the world have contributed.

Satloff: Thank you, Ambassador al-Reedy. Moshe, what do you see as the objective of the campaign against terrorism?

Moshe Arens: The objective is crystal clear: most immediately, to prevent a recurrence of what happened on September 11 and, in the wider sense, to prevent an occurrence of such an event anywhere else in the world. There should be no doubt or mixed feelings about what needs to be accomplished. The president of the United States is determined and resolute, fixed exactly on that objective, and we have every reason to believe that this objective will be attained.

Satloff: Gilles, how do you interpret the objectives of the coalition?

Gilles Andréani: Mr. Arens stated them very well. They may be broken down in operational terms under a few headings: dismantle the Taliban regime, install a broad-based government in Kabul, eliminate al-Qaeda, and destroy the perpetrators of the September 11 attacks. There is wide agreement on these objectives, as well as day-to-day cooperation toward achieving them.

Satloff: Dennis, how do you interpret the president's call for a campaign against terrorism?

Dennis B. Ross: The president defined the objectives clearly when he stated that this is a war on terror. Prior to September 11, our objective was always to counter terror. Now it is to defeat terror. He has also made it clear that the ultimate measure of that defeat includes not only destroying the network, but also ensuring that these groups no longer have a place from which to operate. In other words, we must deprive them of the luxury of being able to plan, organize, recruit, and finance. We must make sure they are worried about whether someone is coming after them—either because they no longer have a sanctuary, or because they are so preoccupied with their own security that they are less capable of posing a threat to anyone else.

In a nutshell, the president has defined the war on terror in unlimited terms. He made clear that we will be consistently working both unilaterally and collectively to ensure that there is no safe haven, no harbor, no capacity for these groups to continue to plan and carry out attacks. We hear about Phase I and Phase II, but in a sense the president has established a comprehensive set of objectives—even though the strategy and tactics could be sequential. Stopping with Phase I would be inconsistent with the objectives he has established.

Satloff: Given the sets of objectives you have each defined, let us consider the role played by each of your countries in this coalition. Gilles, please begin with France specifically, then Europe more generally.

Andréani: You are right to mention the breadth of the dilemma, because this is not just a French or British or German problem. Indeed, one of the most significant responses to America's call for action has been the decision by heads of state in the European Union to put into place better extradition procedures for terror suspects.

For example, we have had two waves of major terrorist attacks in France, one in the mid-1980s sponsored by Iran, and one carried out by the Armed Islamic Group (GIA) in the mid-1990s, not unlike the sort carried out by al-Qaeda. Since 1995, we have sought the extradition from Britain of a terrorist that we suspect is the main financial arm behind the terror wave of the 1990s. To this day, he has yet to be extradited from Britain, not because of bad political will, but because the system is so complex. We need a qualitatively different kind of cooperation among the police, judiciary, and intelligence services. Progress is being made within Europe and between Europe and the United States, and there is now a commitment to dramatically increase the level of cooperation. This kind of effort does not make the headlines, but it is fundamentally important.

Second, Europe will contribute militarily to this operation. A slight problem faces us in this regard: the Europeans want to contribute literally, while the American military has operational problems integrating this offer into their own planning, due to the complexity of the campaign and the unity of command required. But European leaders and their publics want to contribute troops, aircraft, and whatever else is needed. They perceive that, for the sake of transatlantic relations, a sizable European military component must be involved, even if the Americans do not necessarily need us on the ground.

In the days immediately following the September 11 attacks, 74 percent of the French public was in favor of committing troops to the operation. To date, there may be two French ships now under U.S. command in the Indian Ocean, and, reportedly, ongoing negotiations continue on committing special forces and other assets. A more recent survey showed that 55 percent of the French public wants to see greater French participation in the operation. And this is not just a French mood; it is a European mood. Significantly, even the Germans are on the same wavelength, though perhaps not to the same degree as the French. It is conceivable—and to my mind highly desirable—that we may see Germany showing in this operation. It would be an important contribution from a political standpoint.

Al-Reedy: It is very important that this question of extradition be resolved. Dangerous terrorists remain in some Western capitals. Egypt has asked these governments to extradite them, and we have been refused. In the meantime, we see the terrorists giving television interviews, and so on.

Satloff: Is there any intra-European political competition—jealousy that the British prime minister is the public face of the campaign and that the other European leaders are somehow not on the same par in President Bush's estimation?

Andréani: No, this is a serious affair, one in which we perceive our interests to be involved in a number of ways. First, a great many Europeans were killed in these attacks. Second, we cannot live in a world in which people who are dissatisfied with U.S. foreign policy remain free to express themselves in this manner. We have had experience with Islamic terrorism, and it reverberates in our society. It is an issue in which our feelings command that we do something.

The British prime minister contributed to the coalition from the outset with important naval maneuvers in the Gulf of Oman. France will take a little more time to contribute because our forces are not currently in place, and it is difficult for us to acquire the bases from which to operate. But at the end of the day, we will come. There are more important considerations at the moment than trying to sort out who is the best aligned and so on. What America needs is Europe, period, and Europe will be there.

Satloff: Moshe, this is not the Gulf War. Define Israel's role in this coalition. Prime Minister Ariel Sharon has expressed profound concerns about this issue.

Arens: Let me first reemphasize the objective. We do not want a recurrence of what has already happened. Rehavam Ze'evi, an Israeli cabinet minister, was just assassinated—this may not be as dramatic as the horrible events of September 11, but it was, nevertheless, an outrageous act of terror. When we judge this campaign's success, we will do so on the basis of whether terrorism persists. The members of the coalition that put their shoulder to the wheel will include, first of all, those countries that themselves feel threatened. Obviously, Israel continues to be threatened, and we will do whatever we can—not only because we are an ally of the United States, but because it is in our self-interest. In Israel, putting an end to terrorism is the number-one priority.

There is a great difference between the coalition that President Bush is trying to build today and the coalition that his father built ten years ago. In those days, certain Arab countries were essential to the coalition. You could not mount an offensive against Saddam Husayn's forces without the use of bases in Saudi Arabia, and without fielding Gen. Norman Schwarzkopf's 500,000 troops on Saudi Arabian soil. The immediate objective of that campaign was to liberate an Arab country, Kuwait. Other Arab countries felt immediately threatened by Saddam. Saudi Arabia thought, rightly, that it would be next in line if Saddam were not defeated, and President Mubarak, too, felt his rule threatened by the Iraqi leader. The Syrians had a longstanding dispute with Saddam and therefore likely joined the coalition without any trepidation.

Today, the situation is entirely different. Some Arab regimes do not feel directly threatened by Osama bin Laden, and consequently their enthusiasm for joining a coalition may not be as fervent as it was ten years ago. Also, some of the capabilities or bases in these countries are not essential for the job. For the time being at least, it looks like the United States has the ability to do this job on its own, perhaps with the help of Pakistan and possibly Tajikistan and Uzbekistan. Other countries can assist either because, as Gilles suggested, they want to be members of a coalition that will defeat terrorism or because they have abilities that are essential, such as in the field of intelligence. Israeli intelligence services have a reputation for being efficient, so I assume they will be partners in this capacity.

Satloff: Do you believe that Israel's desire to be part of this coalition has been acknowledged sufficiently?

Arens: In many ways, this is a virtual coalition. It is not the kind of coalition made up of countries that actively participated in the campaign against Saddam Husayn ten years ago. I would be surprised if Israel's current intelligence contribution were rejected.

Satloff: Abdul Raouf, again, this is not the Gulf War. We are not asking for Egyptian ground divisions. What is Egypt's role in this coalition?

Al-Reedy: Moshe analyzed the coalition question very well. There is a basic difference between the coalition today and the coalition during the Gulf War. Major officials from the U.S. administration were in Cairo recently, and the Egyptian government agreed to provide cooperation in every area requested: intelligence, information, passage through the Suez Canal, and so on. There were no reservations by the government on any of these points.

Satloff: In your opening comments, you made reference to the fact that in this war, words play a special role. Is Egypt playing its part to the fullest on the issue of what is spoken, what is preached, and what is broadcast via the Egyptian media?

Al-Reedy: You have to differentiate between responsible Egyptian officials who are supporting the coalition on the one hand, and the media, which is analyzing, on the other. In Egypt, there is also an Islamic trend. Some in our society may criticize what is happening in Afghanistan and Pakistan. Indeed, there is a broad spectrum of analysis, and all shades of opinion exist. But this kind of analysis takes place in every part of the world—certainly in the United States, but also in Israel, France, and the rest of Europe.

For instance, we have established the Egyptian Council on Foreign Relations, which provides an open forum for important journalists, members of the business community, and intellectuals. We would like to engage American civil society.

Satloff: We will come back to the question of words. Dennis, what do you think Washington expects from the coalition partners?

Ross: Washington operates on the premise not only of establishing comprehensive objectives in the fight against terrorism, but also of using every instrument of statecraft. First, we need a collective response on the banking issue. Second, there is the question of intelligence. We have to create a common data base, which again must be universal. Third, there is the question of law enforcement, extradition, and the judiciary. This, too, requires a new set of operational standards, so that if we have intelligence about a suspect, we have the ability to act against him or her. Terrorists should not have the ability to move freely across borders.

From the standpoint of all of these functions, everyone is part of the coalition; this kind of cooperation costs no one anything. Consequently, if any one country holds back, the United States will likely put pressure on that government. Even those sensitive about being identified with the United States cannot have a real problem with this kind of cooperation, because it is essentially invisible. U.S. cooperation with the respective governments represented on this panel is something that you can count on as being under way already.

The more complicated element concerns the use of force. As Moshe said, today's situation is completely different from the one that held ten years ago, and, as a result, our requirements are also different. The United States has built up a force, but it is not the same kind as that of 1990–91. We do not have 500,000 troops on the ground. We may have a lot of aircraft, naval forces, and special forces, but it is an entirely different kind of requirement. Pakistan and Uzbekistan are important from the standpoint of hosting some kind of American presence. But Egypt might be important to us logistically: allowing our ships to go through the Suez Canal or loosening overflight requirements. Issues like transit rights and logistics support have varying degrees of visibility. The more visible they are, the more they may raise questions for some of the countries to whom we are talking. For the most part, though, we will not have a problem in Phase I—namely, the eradication of Osama bin Laden and the Taliban. The real test will come in Phase II, when we will find out, effectively, who is committed to the war on terror and who raises certain objections because of their own exposure. The test at this point becomes much more profound.

One last thought touches on the world of ideas. We do not want this campaign to pit the West against Islam. And that kind of polarization is the last thing our friends in the Muslim world should want. It is very much in their interest to be highly active in discrediting this notion. Other issues, if allowed to dominate—including some that I worked on for years—also play into bin Laden's hand. Saddam Husayn invaded Kuwait in 1990 and said, "I did it for the Palestinians." One week after the invasion, I was with President Mubarak when he said, "We are not going to give Saddam that issue." Let's not give Osama bin Laden that issue either. (Applause.)

Al-Reedy: Yes, Mubarak said that Egypt would not allow Saddam Husayn to link his advance against Kuwait to the Palestinian problem. You will remember that we discredited Saddam. But you will also remember that in November 1990, President George H. W. Bush held a press conference in Cairo announcing that the United States would commit to solving the Palestinian problem after the liberation of Kuwait. On that basis we convened the Madrid conference. Now, Arabs look at the current situation in Palestine and see that nothing has been resolved. The best way to take this issue away from Osama bin Laden is by committing to resolve it—in a serious way. Otherwise, you go from one crisis to another, claiming not to be able to move forward on the Palestinian problem because of the question of bin Laden, the Taliban, and so on. Instead, you should do all you can simultaneously to resolve this festering issue.

Satloff: We were operating under a different principle in 1990–91: win the war first and use the credibility of winning to wage peace.

Al-Reedy: Even so, you must send a message to the Arabs—who watch as the Palestinians continue to fall victim to atrocities—that you are serious about solving this problem. It will not detract from your efforts against the Taliban and Osama bin Laden. In fact, doing something about the Palestinian problem is a good way of addressing the latter.

I do not know about Phase II, but let me tell you something. I am from the Arab world; I sit in the cafés of Cairo and I listen to the grievances of my fellow Egyptians. Many intellectuals as well as those in the street note that the Americans have been perpetually bombarding Iraq for the past ten years. Half a million Iraqi children have died; this is not a small number. Why is the life of an Arab worth less than the life of someone from the West or from Israel? You now say you are going to hit Iraq in Phase II—and not just with minor, sporadic bombing. In this, you will have a problem in the Arab world. Who has the authority to determine that Iraq should be hit? I am a friend of the United States, but with all due respect, should this be a unilateral decision? Is it something so serious that it is worth causing—or at least risking—a schism with the Arab and Muslim worlds? At least present evidence and discuss it within a collective framework, so that we do not just wake up one day and see on CNN that Iraq has been hit. This will cause a serious problem.

Arens: I feel uneasy when I hear it said that the acts of terrorism committed on September 11 are, if not excusable, at least understandable, and that there are root causes for these horrendous acts. This kind of talk is not at all helpful in the present campaign. Nothing—nothing—can excuse or justify such acts. This, as President Bush has said, is evil incarnate, and it is unhelpful in such a context to carry on discussions about how we are going to solve the Israeli-Palestinian problem, or how we are going to solve the Kashmir problem. First things first. Let's take care of these guys. (Applause.)

Regarding any attempts that may or may not be made in the coming weeks or months to resolve the Israeli-Palestinian conflict, Dennis Ross and others have spent years attempting not only to bring resolution and moderation to the conflict, but also to address its causes. But the vast majority of Israelis—indeed, of people throughout the world who have been working to resolve this conflict—have concluded that nothing will be accomplished with Yasir Arafat in charge.

Ross: On the issue of linkage, Rob is quite right. It was a sequence: win the war first, then go to peacemaking. Now, Ambassador al-Reedy, you are saying that we should send a message. It would be a lot easier to send a message if we saw a demonstration by the Palestinians and by our Arab friends that they are prepared to assume their own responsibilities. Peacemaking is a two-way street. We do have a responsibility to help promote peace in the region—I have devoted a major part of my life to that task, I still believe in it, and I am not going to walk away from it. But there has to be a climate that makes peacemaking possible. We cannot have people declaring that suicide bombing is a legitimate tool used in the pursuit of a cause. That is not resistance; it is terror. These people are not martyrs; they are monsters. In order to produce a reality in which the world is not polarized between the West and Islam, our friends in the region must make it clear that terror—no matter what the cause—is illegitimate.

You do not have to give up your grievances, your claims, or your aspirations, but do not pursue them through the use of terror, suicide bombing, and the deliberate targeting of civilians. That is wrong. When you in the region make this clear and begin condemning anyone who says otherwise, it will be much easier for us to send the message you just outlined.

Satloff: Assuming that we see early success in Phase I of the campaign against terror, of what will Phase II consist, and what will the coalition look like in that phase?

Arens: If, after a U.S. success against bin Laden and the Taliban, there is a recurrence of terrorism somewhere in the world—even if the United States remains immune to its effects—the campaign cannot be spoken of as a success. Certainly in the president's terms it would not be viewed as a success. Having mobilized the necessary capabilities and achieved momentum, the campaign will continue until terrorism has been struck down everywhere.

In terms of the coalition, it might be useful to ask whether Iraq, Iran, or Syria will become members. I ask because these countries practice terrorism and provide haven to terrorist organizations. It is not difficult to identify terrorism-sponsoring regimes. For example, the headquarters of the Popular Front for the Liberation of Palestine—the group responsible for the assassination of Rehavam Ze'evi—is located in Damascus. Perhaps merely going through the motions of asking the Syrians to join the coalition is not very useful. To the means that Dennis Ross earlier said should be explored you have to add the means that must be exercised against state-sponsored terrorism, which, in many ways, is a great deal more difficult.

Perhaps, under the impact of U.S. successes against the Taliban and Osama bin Laden, Bashar al-Asad will kick all of these terrorist organizations out of his country. Perhaps he will end the operations conducted from Lebanon. Perhaps the Iranians will stop sponsoring Hizballah. If not, the coalition will have to make these things happen.

The U.S. list of most-wanted terrorists includes Imad Mughniyeh, a member of Hizballah. He was responsible for the suicide bombing of the U.S. Marine barracks in Beirut that killed 241 Marines. He is probably also responsible for the suicide bombing of the French soldiers' compound in Beirut, for the bombing of both the Israeli embassy and the Jewish community center in Buenos Aires, and for many other acts of terrorism. Today, Mughniyeh moves easily between Iran, Lebanon, and Syria.

I find it hard to believe that once Phase I is completed, nothing more will be done, leaving a man like Imad Mughniyeh to roam freely. I expect President Bush to translate into action what he has said—that the coalition will bring Mughniyeh to justice or bring justice to him. Bringing justice to him involves holding accountable those countries in which he operates freely. (Applause.)

I do not want to predict what Phase II will look like, but I have no doubt that the states that sponsor terrorism will appear on the agenda. Perhaps—under the impact of the coalition's success in Afghanistan—Iraq, Iran, and Syria will abandon their policies of sponsoring terror. It is unlikely that the United States and the coalition will accept any other position.

Satloff: Gilles, do you think that these are legitimate targets for Phase II?

Andréani: We are using two words, "war" and "coalition, "which we accept because they are part of the debate. But in my mind, Osama bin Laden is not a warrior; he is more of a criminal. Therefore, against bin Laden, "war" may not the best word to use on the propaganda front. We must be conscious of how words color the problem.

Phase II relates to qualitatively different levels of cooperation in the fight against terrorism. We will apply different standards in judging the behavior of certain countries than those that were used in Phase I: Whom do these states harbor? Whom do they help? What funds do they allow to pass through their banking systems, and to whom? Assuming that Phase I is successful, Phase II will primarily consist of applying pressure. But we have made ourselves prisoners of the words we have chosen. We think of Phase II as a question of where the next military operation will take place. That complicates the debate because in many instances—especially if Phase I ends soon—countries will acquiesce and you will not have to wage war on them. They will think twice before resisting outside pressure.

In this context, I do not find it particularly useful to say that Iraq or Iran or Syria is the next target in the "war," because these actors will be greatly influenced by what happens during the months to come. They will succumb when confronted with precise American or Western demands.

Satloff: On the question of criminality versus war, NATO has invoked Article 5 of the Washington Treaty in support of this campaign; it would not invoke this article against criminal activity. In other words, a significant part of the international community has formally recognized that we are in a war situation.

Andréani: This show of solidarity with the United States was well advised. I am speaking more on the level of words and ideas, and I still maintain that there are useful alternatives.

Satloff: Just to press you a bit on Phase II, you suggest that the demonstration effect of Phase I will have a powerful reverberation throughout the world. Assuming complete success in this phase, what group, organization, or state sponsor is least likely to give up its support of or engagement in terrorism?

Andréani: We are in for a surprise in this respect. The attitudes, strategies, and cost calculations of many actors will shift. Look at Pakistan today. It is ironic that Pakistan is the centerpiece of the coalition in the current fight against the Taliban, because we all know that state elements there have more than flirted with terrorism. Of course, they will probably want to have it both ways—they will want to help defeat the Taliban and also keep open some of the options they have used against India, Kashmir, and others.

The tools you will likely see activated in Phase II include pressure, discussion, and the influencing of various actors through a variety of means. This is more likely than open warfare against state "A" or "B."

Ross: Our success against the Taliban will have a consequence, a demonstration effect. When you remove a regime you send an unmistakable message to other regimes that are providing sanctuary, and this may obviate the need to use military force. I suspect that, after succeeding in Phase I, we will be in a position to agree on a stronger set of nonmilitary measures that will squeeze those who provide sanctuary. But at least the threat of military force should be present, in the event that some do not get the message.

Now, if things were to work in a linear fashion, this is all we would need. But the idea that we will have a neat, clean Phase I and then move on to Phase II does not fit the real world. Other events will intrude, and when they do we will have to adjust. For example, what if we find evidence of involvement by a state in the events of September 11? This would change the ground rules of Phase II, because we would have to respond.

One last comment. Some have questioned America's staying power. This was an attack on the United States. If we do not respond, we will be attacked again, and we may be attacked again anyway. We do not have a choice; war was imposed on us.

Satloff: We will now open the floor to questions from the audience.

Participant: Would the United States respond militarily to some future chemical or biological attack?

Ross: We would not necessarily do what we are doing now to the Taliban, but yes, there would be a military response. It would not be that difficult to develop coalition support, because anthrax could be used against any population, not just our own. The threat would be seen and felt widely.

Al-Reedy: If there is evidence of state collusion in such an attack, the United States should discuss the matter multilaterally—possibly in a special meeting of the UN Security Council, whose five permanent members all oppose terrorism and weapons of mass destruction (WMD). When conclusive evidence has been presented, then action can be taken. This is preferable to unilateral action on the part of the United States.

With regard to weapons of mass destruction in the Middle East, we in the region have already declared our support of the need to ban WMD. An initiative to move toward this end, launched by President Mubarak in 1990, was actually adopted by the Security Council in the context of the Iraq crisis. The initiative spoke of the need to eliminate all WMD—biological, chemical, and nuclear—from our volatile region.

Andréani: If any state attacks the United States with biological or chemical weapons, you will find support in Europe, along with whole-hearted cooperation toward punishing that state. Europe collectively stands by the United States on this.

By the way, building and maintaining a coalition requires more than asking a series of academic questions. It is a dynamic process, and priorities—not just a wish list of whom you would like to get rid of—must be set at the outset of each phase. There are plenty of actors whom we would like to see exit the stage, including Saddam Husayn. But to be able to accomplish that objective, to have the means and support, and to act at the right moment—these prerequisites are a matter of politics. Indeed, keeping a coalition together is an extraordinarily difficult task. In the fight against terrorism, how do you convince India that Pakistan should be the centerpiece of the coalition? How do you build on current signals from Iran that they are happy to get rid of the Taliban after all, and that they may even help in some way? Targeting Iran next because we dislike Hizballah has merits, of course, but perhaps it is not the best decision in terms of coalition management.

As a foreign but interested observer, I believe the United States has done very well on the tests that it has encountered thus far; the coalition has been deftly managed. We will agree on some objectives, but there will also be some difficult moments ahead in which we disagree. In the end, however, Europe will stand with you.

Satloff: What is the weakest link in the coalition?

Andréani: There are weak links everywhere. You will push certain countries on the intelligence or legal fronts, for example, and they will not respond. But at the same time, you may need them for on-going operations. Saudi Arabia may provide a good example in this regard.

Arens: Some countries are not enthusiastic about the coalition, or perhaps do not feel a very strong moral obligation. But in the end, almost everything depends on the United States. It is doubtful that any single country would have the capability to unravel the coalition.

Bernard Lewis, *Princeton University:* I fully accept the argument that the coalition needs to solicit the support of Muslim states in order to demonstrate that this war is not against Islam. But in soliciting the support of terrorism-sponsoring states, does one not demonstrate that this is, in fact, a war directed against our own specific adversaries, rather than one directed against terrorism? (Applause.) I can well imagine that a number of these countries are hesitating, asking themselves, "Do I want to help a coalition that needs my help?"

Ross: I am certainly able to restrain my enthusiasm for including terrorism-sponsoring countries in the coalition.

Andréani: Professor Lewis has posed a crucial question. Pakistan, for example, is not—strictly speaking—a terrorism-supporting state, but it has certainly made use of terrorism in its own backyard. As much as we may dislike it, we may have to use a double standard in such cases.

Rep. Howard Berman, *U.S. Congress:* Ambassador al-Reedy, I would like to follow up on your anecdote about sitting in the cafés of Cairo, listening to the expressions of anger and humiliation about Iraqi women and children who are dying of starvation. Do enormous amounts of money not come to Baghdad from the "oil-for-food" program, which is designed to feed those Iraqi women and children? Is Iraq not one of the largest exporters of oil? And is it not true that in the northern areas of Iraq, which are not controlled by Saddam Husayn, no starvation exists because the money that arrives there from the oil-for-food program is quite sufficient to feed the people?

And is it not also true that the moment Saddam allows weapons inspectors back into Iraq, the sanctions will end? In fact, it is Saddam's policies, not those of America or the UN, that are causing the starvation. When you go to those Cairo cafés, do you tell the people that this is, in fact, the reason for the starvation? Is this the message sent by government leaders and the Egyptian media to the people of Egypt? (Applause.)

Al-Reedy: The next time I go to a Cairo café, I will try to explain the complexities of the Security Council oil-for-food resolution to which you are referring. I am not defending Saddam Husayn; we fought him. Before the invasion of Kuwait, Egyptian workers suffered because of him. I am simply telling you how it looks to the Egyptian man in the street.

Some of these starvation reports, by the way, come from your own most reputable institutions, such as Harvard's School of Public Health. The bombing is going on constantly, and when you also see resignations in protest—for instance, by the UN's humanitarian coordinator in Iraq, Denis Halliday—the statistics have more credibility. The starvation of Iraqi children might be Saddam Husayn's responsibility, but explaining Security Council resolutions to the Egyptian public will not alter their perception that the life of an Arab or Muslim is expendable to the West.

Satloff: Is it not in the eyes of Iraq's leader that lives are expendable, rather than in the eyes of those who are trying to bring change to that country?

Al-Reedy: I am simply reporting how the situation appears to the man in the café or to one who is not sophisticated in international politics.

Fred Lafer, *The Washington Institute:* The Egyptian press is very influential. Why does the press not report—in understandable language—that Saddam Husayn is the responsible party? Why does it not report that food and medicine are getting through, and that this fact has been endorsed by the UN? Such efforts would eradicate some of the hatred and misconceptions otherwise created by headlines in the Egyptian press.

Al-Reedy: I assure you that when responsible Egyptian officials speak on the matter they give the correct story. In addition, the United States has a very active embassy in Cairo with an impressive information and communications center. We in the Egyptian Council on Foreign Relations even invited the American ambassador to meet with prominent members of the Egyptian media in order to explain the American position. We do what we can, but the real message is delivered through the bombing and through the tragic statistics.

Andréani: To a large extent, the public relations battle on this issue has been lost not only in Egypt, but in Western Europe as well. That fact is not sufficiently recognized in the United States. Europeans generally believe that it is the sanctions that kill Iraqi children, not Saddam. Many politicians in France, for example, would state this as fact. It has to do with "sanctions fatigue"; the sanctions have been in place for too long, and as a result people do not want to listen to information anymore. Perhaps the level of constant bombing has also blinded them to factual arguments on this issue.

Similarly, French television coverage of the current campaign in Afghanistan includes a lot of footage from al-Jazeera in which one sees Afghan casualties and officers from Western agencies warning of a pending humanitarian catastrophe. You do not see as much of that in the U.S. media, but you must realize that these pictures appear on European television screens with regularity, and they are influencing our public.

Arens: I am disappointed by this last round of discussion. Surely everyone today—certainly a Western country like France—recognizes that leaders who lead their countries into aggression or into acts of terrorism put their own people in danger. The leaders are the ones responsible, not those who are standing up to them. The war against the evil of terrorism will have to be waged without any "ifs," "ands," or "buts."

Edward Luttwak, *Center for Strategic and International Studies:* The larger members of the coalition are wholly absent from this discussion. There is the Russian Federation, without which the Northern Alliance would have no possibility of achieving victory. The Russian

Federation has asked both publicly and privately that this campaign not end until the Taliban are completely destroyed, humiliated, driven out, and extinguished. There is China. The Chinese refused to support the Pakistanis on September 12–13, when the United States put pressure on Islamabad to alter its Taliban policy by 180 degrees. Like the Russian Federation, the Chinese have asked only that this campaign not end until the Taliban are completely destroyed. Then there is India, which is very much committed to the coalition. The principal organizations operating in Kashmir have been put on the U.S. list of terrorism-supporting countries, and India wants the Pakistanis to be forced to abandon their two-faced policy in this regard.

None of these states are concerned about the issues we are discussing here; nevertheless, it is very clear what terrorism means to them. They will not be involved in hunting down the terrorists who operate "out of area"—that is, those who move from Gaza to an Israeli town or settlement. "Let the Israelis handle them," they say. The same goes for Syria. Objectively, Israel is tolerating Syrian support for terrorism. And if the Israelis are tolerating it, why are we asking the Spanish not to tolerate it, or the Belgians, or the Danes, or other members of the coalition?

Moreover, neither Russia, nor China, nor India is concerned about Arab public opinion, because they do not envisage any possibility of a serious move against Iraq. After all, this is a war against Islamist networks, and from an Islamist point of view, Iraq is not heaven; it is a kind of hell where there are women doctors and such. (Laughter.)

Finally, it is hardly surprising that one might find it difficult to explain in France that Saddam Husayn is in the wrong. The French have sabotaged the sanctions regime against Iraq as official government policy.

Satloff: Moshe, some would suggest, as Edward just did, that Israel has a relatively high tolerance for terrorism and is not going after the sources. How do you respond?

Arens: We are a small country, and the casualties we have been taking are traumatic in nature—very large in proportion to the country's size. We have lost 180 Israelis during the past year. Some suggest that we are not doing enough, but the advice we get on many occasions is to restrain our reaction and not to act disproportionately. Israel certainly takes this counsel into consideration. Hizballah, for example, is an active terrorist organization that has done a great deal of damage. Israel could go after Hizballah, but the group operates under the umbrella of the Syrians; it is not a simple matter. To the extent, however, that now, during a campaign against international terrorism, the Israeli government gets greater support, there will likely be more extensive action.

Andréani: I do not want to open another front on Iraq, so I will not respond to Dr. Luttwak's slightly disparaging comments on where the French have stood on this issue. As to the coalition, yes, there are other important members; I wholeheartedly agree with him. The French will also be there, we are happy to be there, and we hope to do our share.

Todd Stern, *The Washington Institute:* Dennis, to what extent do you think the U.S. government will make resolving the Palestinian-Israeli problem central to progress in the war on terrorism? How much pressure will be brought to bear on Israel in this regard?

Ross: I am against linkage because linkage ends up devaluing both issues. If some coalition members tell us that they will not be a part of the coalition unless we perform on the Arab-Israeli issue, we will simply have fewer coalition members. Moreover, if we send a message to Yasir Arafat that he is critical to the maintenance of the coalition, he is less likely to do what he needs to do. So linkage is not helpful, although I personally believe it is important for us to be active on this issue on its own merits. And I would like to see us become more active.

At first, the attitude of the Bush administration was, essentially, "If Clinton couldn't do it, why should we try?" But as the deterioration continued, they came to the conclusion that their aloofness carried a price. Prior to September 11, they were already thinking of becoming more active. After September 11, that signal came through the president's statement on Palestinian statehood. The administration is basically proposing what it had been talking about before: Tenet first, then Mitchell, and then, somewhere down the road, the resumption of a political process. If this is the posture ultimately taken, then I do not foresee any pressure being applied to Israel. But the key determinant will be the administration's level of sensitivity to the coalition on this issue.

Robert Fromer, *The Washington Institute:* Are there any circumstances under which the United States could justify using tactical nuclear weapons to take out facilities proven to contain chemical or biological weapons?

Ross: I am against the use of tactical nuclear weapons under any circumstances that I can foresee. If we use them, we will cross a threshold that we will later regret. We will legitimize this kind of action, which is not in our interests.

Barbi Weinberg, *The Washington Institute:* Ambassador al-Reedy, if the Palestinian-Israeli issue is the root problem, as you say it is, why has Osama bin Laden instead focused most of his condemnation on the governments of Saudi Arabia and Egypt, mentioning the Palestinians only after September 11?

Al-Reedy: I am sure that Osama bin Laden does not care much about Palestine. Bin Laden wants to conduct an intra-Islamic revolution to bring down the regimes he does not like, installing his own vision of Islam in their place. Essentially, he wants to rule the Arab and Muslim worlds, and it is our duty to stop him. We, too, were victimized by bin Laden before September 11. We should stand together against him in one coalition.

Emile Nakhleh, *Council on Foreign Relations:* Ambassador al-Reedy, I would like you to comment on a number of factors that are driving the radical vision of Islam, and which have created an environment conducive to terrorism carried out in the name of Islam. The first is the failure of modern Muslim leaders and thinkers to offer a counterideology to the radical Islamic groups. The second is the international spread of the conservative Wahhabi brand of Islamic education, financed by Saudi Arabia; moderate Muslims have yet to address this issue. And third is the set of repressive, corrupt regimes in the region that have denied their citizens the right to association and free speech, allowing their media to criticize America and Israel but not the regimes themselves.

Al-Reedy: First, Egypt is known to espouse a moderate interpretation of Islam. Islam is a religion of peace. The Qur'an says that if you kill one person unjustly, it is as if you have killed all of mankind. Moreover, the moderate worldview of Islam tolerates the coexistence of religions. It is true that other schools of Islam, possibly in Saudi Arabia, espouse different interpretations. But even when Egypt was in the most difficult economic circumstances, al-Azhar University, for example, continued to produce moderate Islamic thinkers.

As I have said, our own intellectuals and those from the West must engage in dialogue. We in the Muslim world have not been perfect; we must work harder. But you cannot compare our measures against terrorism to those of Israel. The problem in Israel is that there is a military occupation. Do not forget that. The occupation is not healthy for Israel or for the Arab and Muslim worlds—or for the world in general.

Nakhleh: In Phase II, we will be facing different definitions of terrorism driven by local territorial claims. We will face this challenge with Pakistan, the Philippines, and, of course, in the Middle East. How would you address this definitional problem?

Andréani: You are absolutely right to say that virtually intractable definitional problems exist in dealing with terrorism across the board. Let me mention an experience I had in early 1998. At that time, the Kosovo Liberation Army was, by consensus, a terrorist organization. One year later, its leaders could be seen in Paris, wearing business attire and negotiating with then–U.S. secretary of state Madeleine Albright. So there are very fine lines here, and the answer lies in prioritizing our actions, starting with where it hurts most and then moving down the line.

Satloff: Gentlemen, we are still in the early days of this campaign, but one hopes that the spirit exhibited by this panel is representative of what we will see in the days ahead.

PART EIGHT

September 11 in Historical Perspective

22

Bernard Lewis

I WOULD LIKE TO BEGIN by explaining a profoundly important difference between Middle Eastern and American culture. In the United States, the phrase "that's ancient history" is commonly used to dismiss something as no longer important, relevant, or worthy of serious concern. Young Americans tend to have a truncated view of history, with events such as the Vietnam War regarded as medieval history, the Korean War as ancient history, and World War II as something like archaeology. Middle Easterners have a very different attitude toward history. For them, history is still very much alive and part of their everyday life and identity.

One example of this difference can be found in the rhetoric surrounding the Iran-Iraq War in the 1980s. At the time, the *Economist* described the conflict as a "squalid war between two barely distinguishable four-letter countries." This is a stark contrast to the grandiose propaganda produced by these two Middle Eastern countries during the war, which contained frequent allusions to Yazid, Hussein, Qadisiyya, and Karbala—that is, to personalities and events of the seventh century. These allusions were not lengthy descriptions of the particular personalities and events, but simple, rapid, incomplete references that were made with the certain knowledge that they would be understood by their target audience, a fair proportion of whom were illiterate. Can you imagine American or Western European politicians attempting to drive their points home by referring to the seventh-century Anglo-Saxon Heptarchy? Of course not. But Middle Eastern societies are surrounded with living history, and the memory of past events is renewed daily, absorbed from schools, from mosques, from entertainment, from conversations. This history may not always be accurate or unbiased, but it is profoundly felt.

Another example of this phenomenon is Osama bin Laden, who frequently refers to history in his public statements. In one recent statement, he alluded to an event that happened over eighty years ago, without going into detail, knowing that his audience would understand. In other statements, he has alluded to medieval and early Islamic history in a similarly casual fashion.

One way of understanding these differing perceptions of history is to look at cultural identity. Westerners are accustomed to history that is divided by country: the history of France, the history of England, the history of the United States, and so on. In Middle Eastern countries, such histories are a very recent phenomenon, still imperfectly absorbed. This should come as no surprise; although most of these countries are in one sense the most ancient in the world, in another sense they are new, rather artificial creations. This fact is reflected in their names, many of which are either borrowed from elsewhere (e.g., Syria, Palestine, and Libya come from the administrative geography of the Roman Empire) or invented (e.g., the name Pakistan, or "land of the pure," was created only a few years before the country itself).

Moreover, while Westerners think of their nations as subdivided into religions, Middle Easterners think of their religion as subdivided into nations. In European historiography, for example, the long invasions of Europe by Arabs and by Turks are always described as just that: wars with "the Arabs" (or "Moors" or "Saracens") and "the Turks." In the immensely rich and varied pre-modern Arabic and Turkish historiography of those wars, however, I have yet to come across a single instance in which they defined their side as "the Arabs" or "the Turks." Their side was always Islam—"the armies of Islam," "the rulers of Islam," "the soldiers of Islam"—and the Europeans, while sometimes designated by ethnic or territorial titles, were more often simply "the infidels." To them, all of these wars were part of the same conflict: the true believers versus the unbelievers. I am not saying that this view is common today, although obviously it still holds for some. It does remain the traditional approach to such conflicts, however, one that is deeply rooted in the historiographical literature. Islam is still a primary source of identity in the Middle East, even among those who are not particularly rigid in their religious beliefs. In this sense, a Muslim might identify more with a fellow Muslim who lives in another country than with his Christian or Jewish next-door neighbor.

The decisive changes that took place in the nature and scope of terrorism can be traced to 1990, when Osama bin Laden became

active and formed al-Qaeda. Bin Laden himself has been very helpful
in explaining the historical roots of these changes. He writes with
remarkable clarity and frankness. We may accuse him of being many
things, but rarely a liar or a hypocrite; he says what he means, often
powerfully and effectively. In his early *fatwa* against the United States,
he describes the jihad against Americans as a defensive one. In his
view, Islam is under attack by infidels, as evidenced by the "occupation," as he sees it, of part of Arabia by American troops, or
"Crusaders." For Muslims, the "Holy Land" is the country where the
prophet Muhammad was born, brought his message, and died: that
is, northern Arabia. Thus, the American presence in part of this holy
land is profoundly shocking to bin Laden and others like him.

When the original Crusaders captured their own holy city of
Jerusalem, the immediate reaction of the Islamic world was minimal.
Arabs in Jerusalem appealed to neighboring Arab rulers for help, but
there was virtually no response. Even the great Saladin, who eventually led the anti-Crusade, was willing to make a deal with the Crusader
king of Jerusalem. The anti-Crusade did not begin until a Crusader
chieftain based in what is now Jordan raided Arabia, attacking the
Hijaz, pilgrim caravans, and shipping in the Red Sea—a raid not on
the Christian or Jewish holy land, but on the Muslim holy land.

Even the British Empire, at its height of power, was careful not to
infringe on this territory. The British nibbled at the edges—Kuwait,
Oman, Aden—but they always stopped shy of entering the Hijaz, which
contained Mecca and Medina. American troops were the first since the
Crusaders to enter the Arabian mainland, with rather similar results.

The roots of the bin Laden phenomenon can also be found in
the modern history of the Middle East, which most historians, including Middle Easterners, agree began in 1798. In that year, a young
French general named Napoleon Bonaparte arrived in Egypt with a
small expeditionary force, quickly conquering the country and ruling it for several years thereafter. This was a terrible shock for Muslims,
who had, even at that late stage, tended to think of the Islamic world
as inviolate. Napoleon demonstrated that even a small European army
could invade, occupy, and rule part of the heartland of the Islamic
world—Egypt, so near to the holy land—with impunity.

The second shock came a few years later with Napoleon's depar-
ture. The eviction of the French from Egypt was accomplished not

by the Egyptians, nor by their suzerains at that time, the Ottoman Turks; it was accomplished by a small squadron of the British Royal Navy, commanded by a young admiral named Horatio Nelson. So not only could a European power invade and occupy the Middle Eastern heartland at will, but it would seem that only another European power could oust those armies.

This was the beginning of some 200 years of history during which the Middle East, even while still nominally independent, was at the mercy of outside powers. Initially, when the greatest powers in the world were the Christian powers of Europe, it was the play of their rivalries and wars that determined the course of events in the Middle East. Middle Easterners learned how to play these powers against one another rather quickly, of course. During the next two centuries, this scenario changed very little, though the players sometimes switched roles: England against France; England and France against Russia; England, France, and Russia against Germany; and so on. In the last chapter of this drama, the rivals were the two superpowers, the United States and the Soviet Union, facing each other in much the same way that Bonaparte and Nelson had, but with much better weapons and on a much larger scale.

Then, something extraordinary happened; the modern history of the Middle East, inaugurated by Bonaparte and Nelson, was terminated by Bush and Gorbachev. Both rival powers checked out of the game—the Russians because they could not play it any longer and the Americans because they would not. Suddenly, the Middle Eastern peoples, and more particularly their governments, had the very disconcerting experience of finding themselves in a totally unfamiliar situation; all of the rules had changed, and they did not know what to do. During the period of Western dominance, particularly the last half of the twentieth century, their strategy had been clear; operating under the principle "the enemy of my enemy is my friend," Middle Easterners had turned to the enemies of Britain, France, and the United States. Between 1933 and 1945, they sought comfort and hope from the Third Reich, and some of their leaders developed very close relationships with the Nazis. After the collapse of the Third Reich, they found that Stalin was a suitable substitute for Hitler. Those who were resisting what they saw as Western exploitation turned very naturally to the new principal enemy of the West, the Soviet Union.

One often hears complaints today about American imperialism in the Middle East. Yet, a closer look at these complaints shows that few are arguing that America is acting imperially. Rather, most critics complain that the post–Cold War United States is failing to live up to its imperial responsibilities, such as settling disputes between Middle Eastern parties. One common accusation is that the United States uses a double standard in the region. But that is most unfair. Why should America be limited to two standards? (Laughter.) A superpower in a world of sovereign powers needs multiple standards for dealing with different situations and entities. Evenhandedness is a desirable and necessary quality for judges, juries, police forces, and other agencies of law enforcement. It would be equally desirable and necessary for an imperial suzerain dealing with various protégés and tributary princes. Yet, as applied to a sovereign power in a world of sovereign powers, the "double standard" charge is utterly meaningless, stemming from a failure to internalize the fact that the old rules no longer apply. The United States is not an imperial power with responsibilities to the Middle East, and it therefore has no particular obligation to be evenhanded.

Osama bin Laden and his followers recognized the new rules. No longer could they play rival powers against each other; if they wanted to continue the struggle against the West, they had to take it into their own hands. This realization was part of the founding logic behind al-Qaeda and its recourse to strategies and weapons that had not been used in the past. Their line of thinking is perhaps best illustrated by a famous line from medieval Islamic poetry—that a lone assassin can defeat a mighty king and all his armies.

But the U.S. experience in Somalia showed that some Middle Eastern perceptions are still mired in the past. As most Americans saw it, U.S. involvement was an act of kindness and charity toward a benighted country going through great difficulties. When the intended beneficiaries proved murderously ungrateful, the natural response was, "To hell with you, we're getting out. We don't need this." Yet, Osama bin Laden perceived the situation differently. In a 1998 interview with ABC News[*], he expressed the not-uncommon interpretation that the United States went to Somalia with predatory, imperialistic intentions. Why anyone in his

---

[*] Printed in *Middle East Quarterly*, vol. 5, no. 4, December 1998, pp. 73–79.

right mind would think that the United States wanted to extend its domain—and hence, responsibilities—to a place like Somalia baffles the
imagination; apparently not the Middle Eastern imagination, though.

The end of the Somalia fiasco illustrates another common perception in the region: that the American invaders were driven out by
force and fled in terror. This perception has contributed to the disre-
spect, as Martin Kramer has pointed out, that many in the Middle
East felt toward the United States when it refrained from taking forceful action against terrorism. The 1979 hostage crisis in Iran further
illustrates this phenomenon. Articles written by the hostage takers
and published in the Iranian press in years subsequent to the crisis
revealed that when they seized the embassy hostages, they intended
to hold them for only a few days and then let them go. When they
saw the response from Washington, however, they decided that they
were on to a good thing—at least until Ronald Reagan came along.
Reagan's election convinced them that further protraction of the crisis could be dangerous. As one of them said at the time, "This man is
like a cowboy who will come out with his six-shooters." So they released the hostages before Reagan even took office.

Another lesson from the hostage crisis is that it occurred not
because relations between the new government of Iran and the United
States were deteriorating, but rather because they were improving.
Days before the crisis, a meeting took place in Algiers between the
relatively moderate Iranian prime minister Mehdi Bazargan and the
U.S. national security advisor Zbigniew Brzezinski. A photograph of
the two men shaking hands was highlighted by media across the world,
including the Iranian press. For the less moderate forces in Iran, this
was a real danger sign. They needed the United States as an enemy,
so they provoked the assault on the embassy. After all, having the
United States as an enemy gives one dignity and stature.

Undoubtedly, there is much hatred in the Middle East for the
United States; it has been growing for a long time and for a variety of
reasons. Yet, the real danger lies in the fact that this hatred is no
longer tempered by respect or constrained by fear. Still, it is important to ask why this hatred exists. One answer lies in the long list of
specific grievances issuing from various parts of the Muslim world.
Conflicts between Muslims and non-Muslims are ongoing in several
areas of the globe—Chechnya, Bosnia, Mindanao, Kashmir, and so

on. The most prominent and frequently cited of these conflicts is that which exists between the Arabs and Israelis. Of course, this is a serious conflict; however, its prominence is due largely to the fact that among the many grievances felt by citizens of Arab countries, it is the only one that can be freely and safely aired. Thus, the conflict serves as an invaluable safety valve for other, much more dangerous problems. This is not to underrate the importance of specific Arab grievances against the West. Nevertheless, the underlying problems within Arab countries are greater than these grievances, and I doubt that remedying any specific grievance would bring significant change.

Perhaps the most important grievance among Middle Easterners—not so much against the United States as against the West in general and against history—is that their civilization has failed in every one of its efforts to keep up with the West. They have tried modernization and reform of various kinds without success. Not surprisingly, it has been difficult for them to stomach the fact that what had for many centuries been the most advanced, creative, and enlightened civilization in the world suddenly found itself outpaced and outperformed in almost every significant field of human endeavor by the upstart, barbarian infidels of the Western world.

Middle Easterners have tried to find various explanations and remedies for this fact. The most obvious remedy was to discover the secret of Western power in order to adopt it. They started with the military, adopting Western weapons, uniforms, organizations, and so forth. Yet, this military Westernization simply led them to defeat after defeat on virtually every battlefield.

Then, they turned their attention to the Western economic system—industry in particular. They tried to modernize their economies, but succeeded only in producing a collection of derelict, bankrupt, impoverished societies.

Finally, they looked to Western systems of government. The trappings of democracy—constitutions, elected assemblies, and so forth—were all very strange to them, and therefore more likely to be the secret talisman of Western success. Yet, when they tried to adopt these trappings, the result was a series of shabby tyrannies and tame assemblies. Over the last fifty years or so, the two dominant political ideologies in the Middle East—nationalism and socialism—have been Western imports as well. Both commanded enthusiastic support in the region, but both have been utterly discredited: socialism by its failure, and nationalism by its success. The Arab world followed various types of socialism, sometimes calling it "scientific socialism," other times "Arab socialism"; they finally decided that socialism is neither scientific nor Arab, particularly since the socialist economies in the region were, for the most part, derelict. The success of nationalism in the region was predicated on a sort of confusion between two different, though related, terms: freedom and independence. For a long time, it was assumed that these two words meant the same thing. Yet, when Middle Easterners achieved independence for their countries, they usually found that they had lost what little personal freedom they already had.

Given these circumstances, it should come as no surprise that many Middle Easterners listen attentively to those who blame the problems in the region on its aping of the West. The alternative that they offer is a return to their roots: to the authentic, God-given message of their faith, and so on. Two serious solutions have become manifest in the Islamic world, embodied in two states. The Islamic solution is ongoing in Iran, where the state is officially grounded on the principle of restoring the holy law as the law of the land. The other solution is one of taking what is best from the West (e.g., free institutions, respect for human rights, responsible government, genuinely free elections) and marrying it with Islamic traditions. This solution is being tried in Turkey, which is experiencing many difficulties, reverses, and upheavals, but is nevertheless making progress.

The Iranian solution has its followers in Turkey, as does the Turkish solution in Iran. In free Turkish elections, Islamist opinions constitute roughly 20 percent of the electorate. We do not know what percentage of the electorate in Iran would prefer a secular democracy, since the expression of that preference is not permitted in an Islamic theocracy. One gets the impression that 20 percent would be a bare minimum, however, and that the real number would probably be much larger.

These, it seems to me, are the two most likely paths that Middle Eastern countries will take in the near future. Which will they choose? Let me conclude by paraphrasing one of Winston Churchill's more famous aphorisms: you can be sure that people will do the right thing after they have exhausted all other possibilities.

23

Discussion

Robert B. Satloff, *The Washington Institute:* Professor Lewis, you ended your account of the Middle East just prior to recent events, with the Soviets leaving the region and America failing to fulfill its "imperial responsibility." But in the wake of September 11, most Americans believe that they have a new reason to take action in that part of the world, particularly in order to root out terrorism. How do you think the region will respond to an America that might indeed have an invigorated sense of mission? If President George W. Bush holds true to his word—of combating both terrorists and the Middle Eastern states that harbor them—what reaction should Americans expect?

Bernard Lewis: In that part of the world, perceptions are all-important. The most crucial factor is not so much what the United States does, but how this action is perceived in the region. Middle Easterners will listen carefully to the various voices coming out of Washington. If what they hear is firm and resolute, they will react one way. If, however, they hear something that seems to reflect fear, uncertainty, or irresolution, they will respond quite differently.

I spoke earlier of the rivalries between Western powers competing for influence in the Middle East. On one occasion, this rivalry took a somewhat different form. Between 1924 and 1926, a bitter war was waged in Arabia between the Hashemites—who were then still ruling the Hijaz—and the House of Saud, who were then ruling in Nejd. In this war, the Hashemites were backed by the British Foreign Office, and Saud was backed by the British India Office. This was seen as evidence of British cunning and duplicity—as their attempt to ensure that whoever won the war would be a British protégé. In London, however, it was seen, I think more accurately, as an extreme form of interdepartmental disagreement. (Laughter.)

Joyce M. Davis, *Knight-Ridder:* If Osama bin Laden is eventually killed during the campaign against terrorism, will Muslims see his death as a modern-day Karbala?

Lewis: From the Shi'i point of view, Karbala describes the martyrdom of one of the earliest heroes of Islam by members of a rival faction. Whether bin Laden's death will be viewed in this manner depends entirely on how and when he is killed, and by whom. His greatest chance of achieving martyrdom is if he is brought to the United States and put on trial, with all of the attendant publicity and mass student demonstrations in his support—and perhaps with a final Supreme Court acquittal ten years later on grounds of insufficient evidence. (Laughter) Whatever the case, simply disposing of Osama bin Laden would not solve the larger and more complex problems that he represents.

One way to combat these larger problems is to help the more-or-less democratic forces that are already operating within Middle Eastern countries. At the very least, the United States should not betray such forces, as was done most appallingly in Iraq. During and after the Gulf War, America called on the Iraqi people to rebel against Saddam Husayn, but then sat and watched while he crushed his opponents north and south, group by group, using the helicopters that he had thoughtfully been permitted to retain under the first ceasefire agreement. This happened again when the United States first gave mild encouragement to—and then abandoned—the Iraqi National Congress, an organization that still offers the possibility of democratic change.

There are democratic movements and individuals in various Middle Eastern countries, and the beginnings of civil society. The United States can certainly do something to help these forces, or at the very least refrain from obstructing them.

Ralph Begleiter, *University of Delaware:* Professor Lewis, you seem to describe a historical pattern in which every time the Muslim world finds itself confronting Western influences, it escalates and alters its efforts to combat those influences. On the basis of this interpretation of the past, what should we expect from the current U.S. involvement in the region? Will it cause further escalation, another attempt by the Muslim world to combat Western influence? Or will this current episode somehow break the cycle and change the pattern of history?

Lewis: The pattern has not been one in which Muslims are constantly combating Western influence. On the contrary, as I tried to point out, the desired policy of many Muslim countries has been to internalize Western systems, such as open economies, elected legislative assemblies, and so forth.

One of the first books to describe England from a Muslim perspective was written by a man named Mizza Abu Talib, an Iranian who was born in India and wrote in Persian. At one point, he described his visit to the House of Commons, the like of which he had never seen. His opening remarks were rather disrespectful, as he compared the proceedings there to a road lined with trees on each side, their branches crowded with parrots squawking at each other. He went on to explain the purpose of the House of Commons, describing how the boor, benighted English, unlike the Muslims, had not accepted any divine law to guide them and were therefore reduced to the expedient of making laws themselves. His task was to explain the very concept of a legislative assembly to a society in which law is divine, eternal, and unchangeable.

But the Muslim world quickly understood the value of this concept. Time and again, Muslims tried to adopt what they thought was worthy of imitation in Western societies, often succeeding. In many significant respects, the Westernization of the Middle East is irreversible. One can find many examples of Western influence even in the Islamic Republic of Iran, whose elected assembly is unprecedented in Islamic tradition or history. Yet, whom does one blame and attack when these adopted systems go wrong? Such situations place the West in a difficult position, because it is much easier for Middle Easterners to blame outsiders than to blame themselves when things go awry.

Marc Ginsberg, *former U.S. ambassador to Morocco:* With respect to the current situation, where do you see the Arab-Israeli conflict heading?

Lewis: Obviously, the present situation is difficult, but I would not say that it is utterly hopeless. All parties are beginning to realize that an indefinite continuance of the conflict would be utterly fruitless. Palestinians and Arabs in particular are beginning to realize that they have lost again and again by refusing to compromise. They refused the British Commission's recommendation of 1936, which would have given them far better terms than were offered to them later. They refused United Nations compromises over and over again. Sooner or later, such realization will become more general, though probably not in the immediate future.

Alan Makovsky, *House International Relations Committee:* As you pointed out earlier, Osama bin Laden has exhorted Muslims to avenge an early-twentieth-century wrong done to Islam. He does not specify to which event he is referring, though, and analysts have bandied about various possibilities without settling on one. To which event do you think bin Laden was alluding, and why?

Second, why have other Muslim nations failed to adopt Turkey's secular, democratic model?

Lewis: To answer the question about bin Laden's allusion, we must go back some 300 years to another pivotal date: 1699. For a thousand years prior, Islam and Christendom had been locked in an ongoing struggle. Islam and Christianity have one important trait in common that, as far as I know, is not shared by any other religion: each of them believes that it is the fortunate and exclusive possessor of God's truth, His final message to mankind. All religions believe that their truths are universal, but only these two believe that their truths are exclusive—that other religions must either accept these truths or remain incomplete at best, or false at worst.

When two such religions with very similar doctrines are historically connected and geographically adjacent, conflicts between them are inevitable. The millennial conflict between these two religiously defined civilizations began with a great Islamic attack. The Muslims came out of Arabia and conquered what were then the Christian lands of Syria, Palestine, Egypt, and North Africa, eventually moving into Sicily, Spain, Portugal, and even France. In the end, these invasions were repelled. The Muslims came a second time, in the form of the Tatars in Russia, and then a third time, as the Turks conquered the Christian land of Anatolia and the Christian city of Constantinople, later invading Europe from the southeast.

From a historical and global perspective, this millennial conflict was a series of ups and downs for Muslims, but people in those days did not have a global perspective; from their point of view, Islam was steadily advancing. As late as the seventeenth century, Turkish pashas were ruling in Budapest and Belgrade, Turkish armies were besieging Vienna, and Barbary corsairs were raiding the coasts of Europe, as far away as England and Ireland, to carry off human booty for sale in the slave markets of Algiers. Islam was still gaining ground, and it constituted a major threat to Europe.

Then came the second siege of Vienna. The first siege of Vienna had ended in a draw, but the second ended in a crushing defeat for the Turks. Contemporary Ottoman historians, with a level of candor rarely achieved by modern historians in the Middle East, described this siege as "a calamitous defeat, the like of which we have not known since the foundation of the Ottoman state." The defeat was followed by a treaty imposed by the victorious enemy—the 1699 Treaty of Carlowitz.

This defeat also began a debate among the Ottoman political and military elite, one that eventually spread to wider circles in Turkey and elsewhere in the Islamic world. In essence, this debate centered on two questions that Muslims had begun to ask themselves: "What went wrong?" and "What is Christendom doing right?" As I suggested earlier, they identified various causes for their defeat and tried various remedies over time, none of which worked.

A related parenthesis is perhaps appropriate here. One Turkish writer offered a potential remedy that, unfortunately, was never attempted. He found that the principal difference between Western civilization and Islamic civilization was their treatment of women. He said, "How can we hope to equal them when we treat our women as we do? Our body social is like a human body that is paralyzed on one side." A vivid image, but no one acted on it.

The debate continued, but it did nothing to stop the gradual Muslim retreat after 1699. Christian powers steadily advanced on the Islamic world. The French invaded, conquered, and colonized North Africa. The British conquered India and the Middle East. The Dutch conquered Southeast Asia. The final cataclysm came in 1918, with the defeat, dismemberment, and collapse of the Ottoman Empire following World War I. This led to the deposition of the last Ottoman caliph, the abolition of the caliphate itself, and the transfer of a large part of the Middle East—at least all the parts that were deemed worth having—to British, French, and Italian rule.

I have no doubt that this is the event to which Osama bin Laden has been referring—the final stage in the retreat and defeat of the Islamic world and its domination by the imperialist West. He does not dwell on the specifics, but on the mere fact that the Islamic world was conquered, occupied, and parceled out among the Western powers. As far as I am aware, he does not address what he would regard as trivial details: treaties that may have been broken or arrangements that may have been made in the parceling out of Arab lands. To him, the domination of believers by unbelievers is the important factor.

As to your second question, the Turks have succeeded largely because they never lost their independence. Unlike most of the Islamic world, Turkey did not fall under imperial rule, nor was it ever subject to the imperial interference that countries such as Iran experienced. Turkey retained a large measure of its independence immediately after the Ottoman defeat. Mustafa Kemal, later known as Kemal Atatürk, led a military movement that achieved liberation. And Turkey was the only one of the defeated powers in World War I that was able to scrap the treaty imposed by the victorious allies and make new terms satisfactory to itself.

The Turks halted Western encroachment and were therefore able to examine their problems without being distracted by the struggle for independence. This was not so elsewhere in the region. The Turks were able to achieve much better results because they could look at the old "What went wrong?" debate in a more practical, detached, and—most important of all—self-critical manner. When things went wrong in Turkey, the Turks said, "What did we do wrong?" not "Who did this to us?" When people continually ask, "Who did this to us?" they often end up generating neurotic conspiracy theories. When they ask, "What did we do wrong?" the next question is usually, "How do we put it right?"

As to the question of why the Turkish example has not been followed by other Muslim nations, there is no simple answer. In general, though, the Turks and the Arabs have a long history of rather bad relations, which has left Arabs disinclined to take any guidance from their previous Turkish masters. That attitude may change, however.

Howard Berkowitz, *The Washington Institute:* Recently, a great many Islamic scholars and religious leaders have used various interpretations of the Qur'an to either justify or criticize the activities of al-Qaeda or other radical Islamic terrorist groups. Can you give us your own interpretation of what the Qur'an has to say about this sort of violence?

Lewis: Although I am not an authorized interpreter of the Qur'an, I can offer a few thoughts on this issue. Since September 11, a great deal has been said about Islam—some by Muslims, but even more by non-Muslims. On the one hand, we are told that Islam is a religion of love, peace, and compassion, rather like the Quakers, but less aggressive. (Laughter.) On the other hand, we are told that Islam is a religion of bloodthirsty barbarians who understand nothing but violence. The truth is in its usual place, somewhere between the two.

Islam encompasses more than a billion people, more than fourteen centuries of history, fifty-six sovereign countries, sizeable minorities in many non-Muslim countries, and an immensely rich and varied civilization. Thus, it is difficult—even dangerous—to generalize about Islam. Moreover, the Qur'an is holy to Muslims, and holy books have to be handled with care. From the Muslim point of view, the Qur'an is not just divinely inspired, which is more or less the Judeo-Christian approach to scripture; it is literally divine, and therefore eternal and unchangeable. Yet, the keepers of the holy law can work wonders with interpretation. Just as American lawyers can offer myriad readings of sacred texts like the Constitution, Muslim jurists are quite skillful in handling their own sacred text.

As for the specific question of where the Qur'an stands on violence, let it first be said that Islam is not a pacifist religion. Muslims are not commanded to "turn the other cheek," nor is there any expectation that they beat their swords into plowshares. This is not part of Muslim scripture. Their attitude, as expressed in their holy writings, is somewhat more pragmatic. In practice, of course, there is very little difference between the historical record of Islam and Christianity when it comes to violence. Both waged holy wars, and Muslims were generally more tolerant of people of other faiths.

In Islamic doctrine, however, the waging of holy war is a religious obligation. The word "jihad" literally means "striving." The Qur'anic phrase is "striving in the path of God." Some early and more modern scholars interpret this in a moral and ethical sense, as striving for one's betterment. The classical texts do not favor this interpretation, though. All of the classical versions of the holy law include a chapter on jihad, dealing with matters such as the opening of hostilities, the conduct of hostilities, the termination of hostilities, the treatment of prisoners, the use of weapons, and the sharing of booty, which are hardly elements of moral striving.

Precisely because jihad is a religious obligation, it is elaborately regulated. The Crusades were not a part of Christian teachings, and were thus unregulated. Jihad is part of Muslim teaching, though, and the laws of war are set forth in considerable detail. These laws categorically forbid ill treatment or indiscriminate slaughter of non-combatants. They demand proper care of prisoners, respect for women, children, and the elderly. They also discuss what weapons may or may not be used.

Some medieval Islamic texts even discuss missile and chemical warfare. The former included weapons such as catapults and projectile clay pots filled with explosive fluids. There were differences of opinion concerning the use of missile weapons—some said they were forbidden, others said they were not, and still others said that they could only be used with care or under special circumstances. Chemical warfare tactics—such as using poison-tipped arrows or poisoning the enemy's water supply—met with general disapproval and were rarely used.

One thing is absolutely clear from classical Islamic law—the kind of indiscriminate mass slaughter seen on September 11 is totally alien to Muslim tradition in all of its different forms. Not until fairly recently do we find certain Muslims attempting to reinterpret the ancient texts in a manner that permits such civilian slaughter. This interpretation is quite new and still very much a minority view in the Muslim world.

Mamoun Fandy, *National Defense University:* Do you think that empires should consult with the pashas under their dominion, or simply give them orders to fulfill? That is, do you think that the United States is uncomfortable with the prospect of assuming the imperial role and imposing its will on Middle Eastern leaders?

Lewis: We must distinguish carefully between imperial and nonimperial situations. A real imperial power may find it convenient—as the British did in India and the French in North Africa—to allow certain native princes to exercise a carefully limited and defined authority within their own domains. This system seemed to have functioned pretty well in various places for quite a long time, but it is not really applicable to U.S. policy in the Middle East. America is not an imperial overlord dealing with native princes. It is an outside power dealing with sovereign rulers.

The real difficulty for the United States in its relationships with various Middle Eastern leaders is the perception that Washington applies a double standard to the Arab world. This grievance, while rarely mentioned publicly or in diplomatic relations, is discussed frequently in private conversation. Basically, many Arabs feel that the United States uses different standards in formulating policies toward Arab and European countries, respectively. "You don't regard us as civilized human beings," they say. "You embrace tyrants in the Arab world whom you would not tolerate for one moment in the West." For example, President Hafiz al-Asad of Syria massacred dissidents on at least one occasion during his rule, but that did not stop successive U.S. administrations from eagerly courting him. According to this viewpoint, the United States deliberately maintains corrupt, tyrannical rulers in Arab countries because it suits American interests to have them in power.

In Arab eyes, the worst case of such behavior is America's record in Iraq. Many Arabs expected the victorious Gulf War coalition to remove Saddam Husayn from power and replace his regime with a new government. Yet, they rapidly began to suspect that the United States wanted a coup d'etat, not a revolution; that is, rather than replacing the tyrant with a popular government, the United States was looking to replace a hostile tyrant with a more amenable tyrant, one who would take his place in the U.S. coalition of tyrants.

Obviously, this approach will not win America any goodwill among Middle Easterners. Although it may serve as a convenient short-term buttress, such a strategy would be disastrous in the long run. What is the alternative to this strategy? The United States could cultivate existing democratic movements in the region, which would be a long and difficult process. Currently, only one Arab country—Iraq—has an organized, effective opposition capable of assuming power, and the West has repeatedly slighted, betrayed, and maligned this movement during the last ten years.

Satloff: What is your view on the longevity of the Saudi regime? This topic has generated considerable debate recently, with some arguing that the regime is on its way out, and others claiming that the House of Saud has far more staying power than most people imagine.

Lewis: Although my professional skills relate to the past, I do not mind predicting the long-term future, as the latter is quite safe. The immediate future is rather more hazardous. When a historian is asked about the future, he cannot with much legitimacy predict what will happen; he can, however, formulate alternatives.

These, then, are the possibilities for Saudi Arabia: 1) the present regime staggers on, presumably with American help, as its problems become greater and greater; 2) the regime is overthrown by some neat arrangement whereby a similar but more amenable regime takes it place; or 3) the regime is overthrown in a more disorderly manner, and the state collapses. We must remember that Saudi Arabia is not a unified state like some others in the Middle East; it is a loose association of tribes and regions that could easily relapse into chaos.

Satloff: What a wonderful walk through history with one of the great minds of our generation. That was a tour d'horizon as well as a tour de force—thank you, Professor Lewis.